FAITH WILL FIND YOU

JEANANNE OLDHAM

Chasing Kites
publishing

CONTENTS

Dedication	vii
Prologue	1
Absent	5
Abundance	7
Accountability	10
Accusations	13
Affirmations	15
Alibis	18
Ambivalent	21
Anxiety	23
Assumptions	25
Available	27
Battle	29
Better	31
Boundaries	33
Bounty	36
Burdens	39
Calling	42
Clean	45
Compromise	47
Confusion	50
Conviction	55
Covering	57
Cravings	59
Direction	62
Empathy	65
Enough	67
Faith	71
Fear	73
Friendship	75

Future	78
Glory	80
God Cares	83
Gracious	86
Gratitude	89
Grief	92
Grounded and Sane	94
Habit	97
Hatred	99
Hearing God's Voice	101
Home	103
Hostage NO More!	106
Isolation	108
Justify	112
Lean Times	115
Lemonade	117
Motivation	121
Nothing	123
Notice	126
Offended	128
Passion	131
Patience	133
Preparation	136
Presence	139
Raw	141
Rebuke	144
Redemption	146
Reflect, Recall, Remember	148
Rejection	152
Relationship	155
R-E-S-P-E-C-T	159
Restrung	162
Safe and Secure	164
Scars	166
Scattered	169
Seasons	172

Solitude	175
Spin	178
Status	181
Survival	184
Superhero	186
Surrender	188
Transformation	191
Trust	194
Vessel	197
Voices	199
Wait	201
Who Knew?	203
Why?	205
Wide Open Spaces	207
Epilogue	211
Acknowledgments	213
About the Author	217

Copyright © 2019 Jeananne Oldham

All rights reserved. No part of this publication may be reproduced, distributed, or transmitted in any form or by any means, including photocopying, recording, or other electronic or mechanical methods, without the prior written permission of the author, except in the case of brief quotations embodied in critical reviews and certain other noncommercial uses permitted by copyright law.

All Scripture quotations are from The Passion Translation® unless otherwise cited. Copyright © 2017, 2018 by Passion & Fire Ministries, Inc. Used by permission. All rights reserved. ThePassionTranslation.com.

ISBN 13-978-0-9997356-9-5

Eagle Image by OpenClipart-Vectors from Pixabay

This book is dedicated to my grandchildren, Baily, Briley, Cal, Ben, Parker, Rollinson Baby Boy (our rainbow baby) and Lilah Noelle (due in September 2019). Always remember, "You are more than enough! Never doubt that!" I am not looking to leave a legacy for you, but an imprint on your heart and life that Jesus is the answer, the key to your present and future always, the hope of forgiveness for anything in your past. Dance like nobody's watching. Sing like a Rockstar. Soar like the eagles and never look back. May each of you have a life as full of the happiness that you have brought me.

"Children are God's love-gift; they are heaven's generous reward" (Psalm 127:3).

Love you FOREVER and a Day!

Mimi

(Picture with Grandbabies) Kacey Stringer Photography

PROLOGUE

As the daughter of a school teacher in rural Louisiana, I too became a teacher. Not because I really knew my purpose in life back then, but because it would give me summers off with my children and it just seemed logical. Living in Oak Grove, Louisiana didn't give us a lot of options for careers. We had teachers and farmers and pipeliners and factory workers. There was also downtown retail or banking. Those were pretty much our choices. I tried retail at Merle Norman Cosmetics and banking at West Carroll National Bank but went back to college once my second child was born.

When I began college at Northeast Louisiana University (NLU), I was seventeen years young and the baby of my family. I dropped out after my freshman year and got married. I was most interested in my MRS degree since I was unclear about what I wanted to be when I grew up. I knew for sure I wanted to be a wife and a mother. Inexperienced in life in general, and somewhat spoiled, after three years of teaching and nine years of marriage, I found myself as a single mother of 3 children back in college working on my master's degree also at NLU.

While looking for a part-time job, I interviewed at a bank chain in Monroe called Central Bank. The interview went well. Part two was writing a letter to a customer given certain criteria and a bank flyer. They were impressed with my letter, telling me it was the best they had ever gotten. However, since my ex-husband and I had filed bankruptcy and I had poor credit, I was declined the job. I remembered this experience as I prepared the edits of this book. I wasn't sure why, but I felt that God wanted me to share it. My skill with writing back then was a glimpse of the talent he would use, but the job at the bank was not my appointment.

Divine appointments are real. Real to me and real to those who have a deep faith in God and what He can do in our lives. The building of our faith comes in a variety of ways. Mine came to a head when I lost my father, Marvin N. Oldham, Sr., in 2013. It was then when I began to realize how out of balance and out of control my life had become. Tragedy and other events in my life sent me floundering and spiraling out of control mentally. I felt hopeless and unworthy. Although I believed in God and was saved and baptized at a young age, I had wandered far away from living a Christian life. I was lost.

It may seem strange to think that tragedies or failures or disappointments are blessings that build our faith, but that's what happened to me. Traumatic events cause us to reflect and think about why we are here. What we are doing and where we are headed. Me, I was headed straight to hell. I found help. In a Christian counselor, I found hope. In my Lord and in my church, I found peace. Through my losses, I found grace. From good friends and family and my Heavenly Father. We are all given the opportunity to be saved by grace.

All the mistakes of my past were forgiven with his mercy, and I began to see a new life within my mind. One that I am now living out by sharing my many hurts so that others can relate. Sharing so that others can find hope and faith through their unexpected blessings of this life.

"Then he broke through and transformed all my wailing into a whirling dance of ecstatic praise! He has torn the veil and lifted from me the sad heaviness of mourning. He wrapped me in the glory garments of gladness" (Psalm 30:11).

My Daddy and his baby girl (2004)

ABSENT

We have all taken people for granted in our lives. We have no idea how long they will be a part of our life. Sometimes we treat them as if they will always be around. We may not call or see them very often. We tell ourselves we are too busy and we'll get around to it later. They are there and then one day you wake up and they are gone.

This happens through a variety of ways—death, physical separation like moving, the ending of a relationship (marriage, friendship, or love interest). Sometimes we know separation is likely when a loved one who has been ill for a while passes away. Other times, someone seems to be doing fine, then experiences a fall or sudden illness and they slip away without us ever considering that ending. Regret follows . . . I should have visited or called more often. We long for more time with those we took for granted. But it is too late. Over and over again, we have conversations at funerals and wakes about how we are going to get together with our friends and family and spend some quality time together before we see them again in this setting. Then BAM! Just like that, we are seeing them again at another wake, and we have never called or gotten in touch in any way. Why?

Everyone needs someone in their corner. But sometimes the person in your corner changes—you wake up one day and they are absent from your life. It's painful, it hurts, and yes, it takes time to regroup and figure out how you are going to move on without crying every day. They say absence makes the heart grow fonder. Sometimes just the opposite is true.

WHO IS THE NUMBER ONE PERSON IN YOUR CORNER? IF IT IS not Jesus Christ, please reconsider the placement of people in your closest circle. Make Him number one today. Will you?

Silhouette by Nancy Bell Art

ABUNDANCE

I sit enjoying the great outdoors in the quiet of the evening alone, but certainly NOT lonely. It has always been such comfort to hear crickets chirp, maybe because it reminds me of church camp days, of screened-in cabins in Pollock or the song that forever rings in my head, "Birds singing their love songs and the lightning bugs are flashing off and on, (*hum*) just sharing the night together." It was a time of long, long ago and that melody still warms me. I am so very blessed—more so than I ever deserve. I feel the abundant love and peace and joy of our Lord Jesus Christ.

I am feeling especially blessed today. Glad to be back in my element. Glad to be back in rhythm with what and where God called me—Jonesboro-Hodge Elementary. I have not seen many of my coworkers all summer or maybe just once. Of course, that excludes Facebook. Duh! What a feeling to have these strong, creative, and talented women and men in my life. Oh, the joys, laughter, and hugs of seeing each other again. I am so very blessed with such incredible educators at my school and in our district.

You must have a passion and calling to stick it out in

education these days. It is not what it used to be—back when my mother taught school. We have new curricula in all contents, and sadly, family dynamics are not what they used to be. As they say, this job is not for the faint of heart. All in all, we still consider ourselves certainly blessed.

With all the things that have changed over time, one thing remains the same—educators. I use that term broadly to include all faculty and staff, custodial, cafeteria, paraprofessionals, office, and teachers—have a heart for our students and their families. They would do anything to help them. And they do. We have parents who continually go above and beyond to help students who are less fortunate. Our community at large is a great supporter of our efforts to make a difference in the lives of our children.

In Proverbs 3:9-10, it states, "Honor the Lord with your wealth and with the first fruits of all your produce; then your barns will be filled with plenty, and your vats will be bursting with wine." I think of the talents, compassion, and care our faculty and staff exhibit on a daily basis. It is the fruits of their labor, and it shows. I was reminded of it over the last few days and today especially. People pitching in to help complete schedules and distribution of materials. Some just stopping by to say hello and ask if they can help.

If you have seen my face in the last few days, you have seen me somewhat panicked and concerned that I would never finish what needed to be done before faculty and staff arrive tomorrow and students arrive on Thursday. Yes, it is year five, and it has all been done on time before. Not that I doubted it would come together, but it's a type of adrenaline —the prepping for back-to-school—it's like having a baby. If you remembered what it was like, you might not ever repeat it. That's why most of us have more than one child—the joy of their arrival and life overcomes the labor, right?

Luke 6:38 says, "Give, and it will be given to you. Good measure, pressed down, shaken together, running over, will be put into your lap. For with the measure you use it will be measured back to you."

This is our year. I am claiming miraculous gains. More laughter and joy in the process. I am claiming more success for educators and students and families as well. It is going to be a great year. To everyone who went beyond that which is outside your job description, thank you. You know who you are. You are my people! I am abundantly blessed!

"Not that I am speaking of being in need, for I have learned in whatever situation I am to be content. I know how to be brought low, and I know how to abound. In any and every circumstance, I have learned the secret of facing plenty and hunger, abundance and need. I can do all things through him who strengthens me" (Philippians 4:11-13 ESV).

Do you offer praise and thanksgiving daily for the good in your life? Trust God in your times of trial, but honor him with a grateful heart every day. Are you willing to do more for others even when you are in a dark season? Embrace your people and give thanks always.

ACCOUNTABILITY

As adults, we are all held accountable. In our job, we have responsibilities and our evaluations hold us accountable for what we do and how well we do it. In marriage and in families, we are accountable in that we are charged with being there for one another in good times and bad. Equally, we are accountable to God.

Romans 14:12 says, "So then each of us shall give account of himself to God."

This is personal accountability. We answer to God and not to man. For this reason, we are to believe we are who God says we are. He is the only One who truly knows our heart and mind and the intent of our actions. It is important that every believer have at least one person in which to confide, pray with, listen, and encourage. Relationships cannot be all take, take, take. There must be a give *and* take. Just as it is important to have someone we can confide in, we also need to be that person for someone else. It is necessary to encourage each other to grow spiritually.

Hebrews 10:24 says, "And let us consider how we may spur one another on toward love and good deeds."

1 Thessalonians says to ". . . Encourage one another and build each other up."

Who is your person . . . or persons? I was reading that if you don't have that person, you should intentionally pray about it. Sometimes that person for you becomes the person you were for them. Did you get that? It's called friendship. It is a two-way street. Have you ever had someone say, you never call me? Or every time you call them, they say, "I was just about to call you"—however, the call never comes from their end? Communication runs both ways... being there for one another is that two-way street. It's the same with God—He wants us to be accountable and in contact with Him.

One saying I have read says, "If we only go to God when we have trouble, then we are in trouble." He depends on us to be there for one another, but also to go to Him with not only our requests but with praise and thanksgiving. We as a people, a nation, and as Christians have so much to be thankful for these days. Sure, there's sin all around us, but in Him we have HOPE. We can have JOY. Have FAITH that God will bring you through whatever it is you are facing, friend. Proverbs 3:5-6 reminds us to "Trust in the Lord with all your heart and lean not on your own understanding; In all your ways acknowledge Him, and He shall direct your paths." He is your FOREVER FRIEND. He will never fail nor forsake you. EVER.

I am blessed beyond measure with friends I can count on to pray with and for me. Friends that I reach out to from time to time to check on. Do I fail as a friend, mother, daughter, sister, principal, and person? Well, certainly, I am human. Remember, "Two are better than one, because they have a good return for their work: If one falls down, his friend can help him up . . ." (Ecclesiastes 4:9-10 NKJV).

JEANANNE OLDHAM

Do you offer praise and thanksgiving daily for the good in your life? Trust God in your times of trial, but honor him with a grateful heart every day. Be a real friend to someone today. You will be blessed for blessing someone else.

Praising Hands

ACCUSATIONS

We have all had them. Untruths said or even spread about us. Maybe even a Facebook post that brings unfounded judgment against us—blessings only for those who have a hidden agenda and are not speaking with kind or true words. Accusations, whether true or false, still hurt, like a kick in the stomach or salt in an open wound. The enemy tries to come against us. He wants to disappoint and disturb our positive thoughts, bring us down with the lies about another's purpose or action, and defeat our feelings of joy. However, if we are grounded or founded in the truths of His word, he cannot succeed. If Christ is our Cornerstone, we are stable. We can stand strong.

"So hide all your beloved ones in the sheltered, secret place before your face.

Overshadow them by your glory-presence. Keep them from these accusations, the brutal insults of evil men. Tuck them safely away in the tabernacle where you dwell" (Psalm 31:20).

I love the message of "The Breakup Song" by Francesca Battistelli. The chorus tells us what we need to say to the enemy when He is planting doubt and fear in our minds about who we are.

I know I'm strong
And I am free
Got my own identity
So fear, you will never be welcome here

You are finally free from the slavery of sin and death. There is now no condemnation for you (Romans 8:1–2). All your sins are forgiven (1 John 1:9). All your unrighteousness has been cleansed by the blood of Jesus (1 John 1:7, 9). You are now righteous in my sight with the very righteousness of my perfect Son (Romans 4:5).

You've been saved by grace (Ephesians 2:8). You've been justified by faith (Romans 5:1). You are utterly secure in me; nothing will be able to separate you from my love in Christ Jesus (Romans 8:39). No one is able to snatch you out of my hand (John 10:29). And I will never leave you nor forsake you (Hebrews 13:5).

WHAT FEARS ARE YOU HARBORING TODAY? REMEMBER TODAY that you are who He says you are. Be blessed today by blessing others!

AFFIRMATIONS

Most of us have heard the saying, "You are what you think." However, our thoughts must be turned into actions to affirm what our future holds—our intentions or purpose in life. Affirmations help purify our thoughts and restructure the dynamic of our brains so that we truly begin to think nothing is impossible. The word affirmation comes from the Latin *affirmare*, originally meaning "to make steady, strengthen."

To receive these affirmations, we must verbally express our dreams in order for them to become a reality. We must speak words of truth and positive ambitions into being. One of my favorite verses is, "Because I place my hope in God, I can soar like an eagle, run and not grow weary, walk and not be faint" (Isaiah 40:31).

In 1991, I was living in Monroe, Louisiana, a single mom with three children under the age of eight. I was working at Jesus Good Shepherd Catholic School teaching computer literacy to K-8 students. I was also going to school working on my master's degree in education. It was a trying time all brought on by my misguided and selfish desires. Thankfully, my family and my Jesus have forgiven me for this time in my life. During this time though, I was still looking for answers and comfort through faith. Like the Psalmist David, although I was walking through the valley of the shadow of death, I feared no evil because I knew my God is always with me. Sometimes, when the students were singing in choir class, I would go listen. My favorite song was "On Eagles Wings." I still love it to this day.

> *And He will raise you up on eagle's wings,*
> *Bear you on the breath of dawn,*
> *Make you to shine like the sun,*
> *And hold you in the palm of His Hand.*

The words of this song brought me comfort during a troublesome time. I knew His protection was mine although I was not living as I should have been. I so wanted for Him to raise me up above the adversity in my life. I wanted to hide in the shadows of His faithfulness, but I chose another path. I turned away, but these words affirmed to me that He was always there for me. Always has been, always will be.

When you feel a heavy heart, when you don't know which way to turn, look to the only one who can affirm. Remember to trust in the Lord with ALL your heart and lean not on your own understanding. In all your ways acknowledge Him and He will make your paths straight. Speak truth into your life with His word. Here are just a few. Pick one a day and speak it over your life and live it out that day.

- I receive peace because I set my heart and mind on things above, not earthly things (Colossians 3:1-2).

- I guard my heart because it determines the course of my life (Proverbs 4:23).
- And I trust God <u>at all times</u> because he is my refuge (Psalm 62:8).
- God is able to do immeasurably more in my life than I could ever imagine (Ephesians 3:20).

Where do you find refuge? Is it in music? Praise? Worship? Reading scriptures? Or something else? When you face dark times, find something that brings you up out of the miry clay. He is always there for us. Never doubt that.

ALIBIS

Alibis means to offer an excuse or defense for someone, especially by providing an account of their whereabouts at the time of an alleged act. Synonyms include defense, justification, an explanation, or reason. Unfortunately, most of us have been lied to either by our children, spouse, friend, or significant other. Heck, we even lie to ourselves sometimes. When caught, people try to justify the action or reason. We hear all about alibis on the murder mysteries when someone is in hot water concerning their whereabouts when a crime took place. I heard Tracy Lawrence's song, "Alibis" on the radio. Here's a portion of the chorus:

Alibis and lying eyes and all the best lines,
Lord Knows she's heard them all
She's been cheated on and pushed around and left alone,
Lord Knows what I've put her through

It brought to my mind how we have alibis or reasons why we can't or won't do what God expects us to do. We make excuses or try to defend ourselves. We can't go to church—I mean we love God and all, but that's just not us. Sure, we want to go to heaven, but we can't serve at church because we travel with our job or we just don't have time or we are too tired. We can get very creative as to why we don't do what we know we should be doing.

Luke 9:59-62 says, "To another he said, 'Follow me.' But he said, 'Lord, let me first go and bury my father.' And Jesus said to him, 'Leave the dead to bury their own dead. But as for you, go and proclaim the kingdom of God.' Yet another said, 'I will follow you, Lord, but let me first say farewell to those at my home.' Jesus said to him, 'No one who puts his hand to the plow and looks back is fit for the kingdom of God.'"

I guess this all came together for me when my friend, Billy, posted a picture of a congregation sitting in six or more inches of water in their church. They weren't standing on the chair seats or refusing to enter a flooded building. They did not even turn around and go back home. Instead, they were thankfully seated with their feet in water almost halfway up to their knees. They were thankful they could still enter in. We are spoiled, aren't we?

One Wednesday night last fall, I arrived at church to find all the lights out. I thought maybe we were doing a candle-light service, but it was actually a power outage. It was one of the most special services I have experienced. No one could look around to see what we were doing or how we were praising because it was truly dark.

We want everything to be perfect for us. Like we deserve perfection? We try to justify our alibis. It sounds good to us. But I wonder how it sounds to God. I wonder how it makes Him feel when we make excuses about why we don't serve Him after He paid the ultimate price for us—His one and only son. He gave it all for us. He gave his ONE and ONLY SON. Not much of a sacrifice. Just His all, His everything.

So then, where's the conflict for us? Why can't or won't we give our all to him? He waits patiently on us. I mean, He must have nerves of steel waiting on me alone. Jesus, thank you for never giving up on me. I praise you for revealing to me that no alibi is sufficient. It is a give-and-take relationship. You gave and I took, but now it's time for me to give. Thank you for your correction and my learning in the lessons.

And he said to them, "You are those who justify yourselves before men, but God knows your hearts. For what is exalted among men is an abomination in the sight of God" (Luke 16:15).

IN YOUR LIFE, WHAT DO YOU NEED TO GIVE OR GIVE UP FOR Christ? Do you doubt that He never gives up on you? Please don't! He will NEVER leave or forsake us and just like the prodigal son, He is always waiting with open arms.

AMBIVALENT

Ambivalence occurs in intimate relationships when there is a coexistence of opposing emotions and desires toward the other person that creates uncertainty about being in the relationship. We have all experienced love and affection that was not returned.

A chronic pattern of ambivalence typically generates a dynamic in relationships where one partner is identified as uncommitted and the other as wanting commitment. Each partner will develop behaviors around this conflict in an attempt to pull their partner closer or push them away. Each partner is expressing a particular role in the conflict over being in the relationship or out of it, but essentially both partners are creating the ambivalent tension between them by identifying with one end of the polarity.

"Just make sure you ask empowered by confident faith without doubting that you will receive. For the ambivalent person believes one minute and doubts the next. When you are undecided, you become like the rough seas driven and tossed by the wind. You're up one minute and down the next. When you are half-hearted and wavering, it leaves you unstable. Can you really expect to receive anything from the Lord when you're in that condition" (James 1:6-8)?

WHAT CHANGES CAN YOU MAKE TO BE MORE CONFIDENT IN what is coming your way? Don't be a doubter. Believe in God's word and be a doer of his word. The storms will come, but the calm is found in your faith.

ANXIETY

If you haven't listened to any messages from Jenn or Brian Johnson of Bethel church, look them up at https://www.bethel.com/. I found one recently on "Overcoming Anxiety" by Brian. This is my take away from his message:

How do you deal with pain? Hurt? Betrayal? Stress? Do you talk to someone about it? Do you cry about it? OR do you stuff it down deep and try to keep it a secret from everyone, including God? We spend most of our time avoiding pain than acknowledging it. We are designed to feel our pain and then bring it and place it at our Father's feet. We should consider it a gift when we reach a point where God is our only hope. That's when our faith grows. That's when we come down to dealing with what we have been stuffing away. That's when our only option is to give it to Him. He should not be our last resort.

Philippians 1:9 says, "I continue to pray for your love to

grow and increase beyond measure, bringing you into the rich revelation of spiritual insight in all things." The only way to achieve this is to have alone time with God. Is what you're doing each morning routine or relational? Our alone time with God should mimic that of being alone on a desert island. Our time with him should be on a friendship level, not a check-done kind of list.

We all have a need for man's approval. But are we getting our kudos and confidence from man or God?

John 5:34 tells us, "¹ have no need to be validated by men, but I'm saying these things so that you will *believe* and be rescued." We are not lifted by praises of men, so then we are not taken down by their insults. Every day we need to offload the garbage in quiet with Him. Our confidence in God is what gives us a backbone. Never forget that any awesomeness we have comes from God, not us.

Be in touch with your feelings. It's okay to feel and face pain because it changes and frees you. Start to make steps toward healing. Get out of the rut and in the rhythm (my theme of the week) of loving God and getting to know who He is. Have faith in who he is and the power of prayer and how it can change your life.

Faith is an inner confidence that God above is enough.

— *BRIAN SIMMONS*

WHAT GIVES YOU THE ASSURANCE YOU NEED TO REMAIN positive? What gives you the confidence to make the changes you need to come out of that rut? Whom do you find your strength in?

ASSUMPTIONS

There is a saying about assumptions. You know it! "Don't assume because you'll make an . . ." You get the picture. We think we know what people think about us or know what we are thinking, when they actually don't. And vice versa. We make assumptions about what others mean without actually hearing what they say. We make an assumption without clarification.

We are the only ones who know what we are thinking unless we tell others. People can't read our minds. Instead, they typically read our expressions or body language. Sometimes we are busy and are really unavailable. In a male-female relationship, folks will tell you to not make yourself too available. I am not good with mind games and don't play them well. I am who and what I am. I am transparent. I am honest, sometimes to a fault.

We speak of availability in our relationships. Are we making ourselves available to our Heavenly Father? Are we sometimes unavailable when He is trying to speak to us or get our attention? Isaiah 6:8 NIV says, "And I heard the voice of the Lord saying, 'Whom shall I send, and who will go for us?' Then I said, 'Here am I! Send me.'"

Are we available to the call that He is making on our life? Or do we make excuses about how we are not qualified? Or do we say, "That's just not me?" Romans 14:12 reminds us that each of us will give an account of himself to God. And then (one of my favorite reminders) there is Philippians 4:13 ESV, "I can do all things through him who strengthens me."

Remember, God does not call the qualified; He qualifies the called.

When I was walking through some of my darkest times, I made one of my best decisions ever—to continue to serve at church. What's the saying—Fake it 'til you make it! It kind of applies. It's like praying when you don't have the strength to fight anymore. It's like singing those songs even when there are tears running down your face—sometimes tears of joy and sometimes tears of pain. Either way, you can't go wrong being available to God at all times. He seeks us out. He wants an intimate relationship with us above all else. Won't you become more available to Him?

"FOR WE ARE HIS WORKMANSHIP, CREATED IN CHRIST JESUS for good works, which God prepared beforehand, that we should walk in them" (Ephesians 2:10).

What can you do to be a more available servant? What have you been putting off in service to Him? Reach out today and step beyond your comfort zone. You won't regret it.

AVAILABLE

No matter what our status says, sometimes we are simply unavailable. Not because we don't want to be, but because of how much our past affects our present and our future. When we don't answer our phone or text—to someone's satisfaction— we are seen as emotionally or even physically unavailable.

We may be only temporarily available or sometimes even unavailable to those we care about the most. This may be due to the wall we build around our hearts. Our fear is being wounded again from hurt or disappointment. It is said that time heals all wounds. I know many of us have come to realize that grief and the absence of someone in our lives can leave a permanent void. It takes time and, yes, sometimes professional help to process those tragic events in our lives that leave us broken or damaged. Once we have taken the proper steps to heal, we work toward moving forward.

It should not be that difficult with Jesus. We should always be available for fellowship with our Father God. He yearns to spend time with us. He wants intimacy with us that only He can satisfy. Making Him a priority in our lives with our time, talents, and service means that we believe His word. Psalm 16:8 says, "Because you are close to me and always available, my confidence will never be shaken, for I experience your wrap-around presence every moment." Because of his availability to us, we can experience the satisfaction that He is forever present in our lives. Tap into the strength, joy, and comfort that being in His presence brings.

Psalm 46:1 reminds us, "... God, you're such a safe and powerful place to find refuge! You're a proven help in time of trouble—*more than enough* and always available whenever I need you." He never fails us or forsakes us. He has given so much for us.

I pray that you will continually experience the immeasurable greatness of God's power made available to you through faith. Then your lives will be an advertisement for this immense power as it works through you! This is the mighty power" (Ephesians 1:19).

WON'T YOU MAKE YOURSELF AVAILABLE TO HIM TODAY AND every day? He is always available to us. He is waiting.

BATTLE

Some say, "Blood is thicker than water." Then why is it that we are not willing to consistently go to battle for the one who shed His blood to save us? He goes to battle for us each and every day. He is behind the scenes fighting our battles when we don't even realize it. He goes before us. He's got our back. He never leaves or forsakes us. He arms us with His word.

Our battles come in all different shapes and sizes. They are so much more than us being wronged. They come at us the hardest in the voices within our minds that tell us what we can't do, what others think of us, what we won't become—happy, content, joyful, blessed, favored. I love the saying, "What others think of you is none of your business." The enemy lies in wait and attacks us in our areas of greatest weakness. He knows us all too well. He strikes in the areas where he has been successful before. In Ephesians 6:16 we are reminded, "In every battle, take faith as your wrap-around shield, for it is able to extinguish the blazing arrows coming at you from the Evil One!" His love and faithfulness are our shield and sword.

One of the best ways to come against Satan is to praise and worship even in the storms and battles of our life. Prayer is another way to combat evil. Pray for wisdom, strength, and courage. "There is only one strong, safe, and secure place for me; it is in God alone and I love him! He's the one who gives me strength and skill for the battle" (Psalm 144:1).

Another way to get our mind off of the attack coming against us is to do for others. What do we do for Him? Are we bold about speaking our faith? Do we serve? Do we tithe? Take a look around you. There are so many others who are suffering, and I mean really suffering, in our world. I don't mean across the nation. I mean next door. I mean your friend or coworker. 1 Thessalonians 5:14 says, "We appeal to you, dear brothers and sisters, to instruct those who are not in their place of battle. *Be skilled* at gently encouraging those who feel themselves inadequate. *Be faithful* to stand your ground. Help the weak to stand again. *Be quick* to demonstrate patience with everyone [italics added]."

"Missing coffee and prayers . . ." My friend, Billy Philley, was laid to rest Sunday, October 7, 2018. The Thursday before was his last post. I overslept and was not feeling well so I quickly skimmed his post and thought what I might comment later that day. I did comment, but he never read it. I say this as a reminder to all of us to say what we want others to know in the here and now because we never know when that opportunity will pass and be our last. Be blessed by blessing others today.

WHAT ARE YOU BATTLING TODAY? CAN YOU LAY IT DOWN and trust God to walk you through to the other side? Yes, you can! How do you fight your battles?

BETTER

Everyone wants better! To be better, to have better, or just to have an overall better life. Have you heard the songs "Better Boat" and "Better Man?" I really like both of them a lot. Then there's the band, Better Than Ezra. I also think of *Better Homes and Gardens* magazine. The trick to being better is one's willingness to change. I love the saying that the definition of insanity is doing the same thing over and over again and expecting different results. All our lives, we have been told, "You can do better than that." The truth is, maybe we can and maybe we can't.

As a Christian, the goal is to become more like Christ. How do we do that? In Romans 12:1-2 we are reminded how to do this: "And do not be conformed to this world, but be transformed by the renewing of your mind, so that you may prove what the will of God is, that which is good and acceptable and perfect. Therefore I urge you, brethren, by the mercies of God, to present your bodies a living and holy sacrifice, acceptable to God, which is your spiritual service of worship."

Another important verse about our transformation to

become better is found in 2 Corinthians 5:17 (NASB), "Therefore if anyone is in Christ, he is a new creature; the old things passed away; behold, new things have come."

This means a total transformation—new thoughts, new actions, new interactions. Do you understand what I mean? It means to trust and obey His word, His teachings, His beliefs; and act accordingly. Jeremiah 29:11 (NASB) says, "'For I know the plans that I have for you,' declares the LORD, 'plans for welfare and not for calamity to give you a future and a hope.'" His plans are better than ours. No matter what we believe will make us happy, keep us content—He knows what is best for us.

No matter what you are going through right now, He has a plan for your life. It is better than what you have now and better than anything you could ever imagine. Hang in there! God is good all the time. He's got your back, for sure!

IS THERE A PERSON YOU THOUGHT YOU WOULD NEVER TALK with again? Maybe they need to hear from you today. Life is short. We never know when our time or those we care about will come to the end of their road. Don't live with regret. Make it right. Always strive to be better not bitter.

Better Boat (by Nancy Bell Waldron)

BOUNDARIES

As I sat listening and watching the rain pour yesterday afternoon, thoughts of how I have changed over the past few years washed over me. I take absolutely no credit for the good changes in me except the fact that I was willing to allow God to make those changes in my heart and life. The experiences of trauma and grief brought me to my knees—literally. They brought me back to God in a way I have never experienced before. I admit I stay grounded in praise and worship music and church more than some understand, but for me, I want to make sure I never slide back into my old habits of thinking or behaving. This is where I need to be.

I felt empty and drained emotionally and spiritually for a long while—pouring myself into others and not refilling my tank so that I could feel refreshed or renewed. Grief overwhelmed me. The loss of my father almost did me in. The end of another failed relationship left me feeling unworthy and ill-equipped to ever have a healthy relationship. But then there's God's word to comfort me.

"The LORD is my chosen portion and my cup; you hold

my lot. The lines have fallen for me in pleasant places; indeed, I have a beautiful inheritance. I bless the LORD who gives me counsel; in the night also my heart instructs me. I have set the LORD always before me; because he is at my right hand, I shall not be shaken" (Psalm 16:5-8 ESV).

Thankfully, I contacted a local counseling center. Please never doubt God's plan for your life. He cares and plans the smallest details of your life. Here's how I know. My counselor, a Christian, God-seeking counselor, helped me bring balance back into my life. She walked me through and encouraged me to come back into fellowship with God. The first book she suggested I read was *Boundaries: When to Say Yes, How to Say No to Take Control of Your Life* by Henry Cloud and John Townsend. I do not believe in coincidences; I believe that God has a well-designed, laid-out plan for my life. I believe finding that counselor was part of the plan to fix my brokenness. I went weekly for a long while and then every other week and then monthly and then just when I needed to check in . . . still. My transformation happened over time. I became more involved in my church, found church friends, increased my faith through additional prayer, reading His word, and of course praise and worship. God has done a work in me and, thank you, Jesus, He is not finished with me yet. For that, I am also forever grateful. He continues to teach me and correct me. Praise God for His goodness and mercy and grace. Amen.

> *"A boundary is simply a property line. It clarifies where you end and the other person begins. You form boundaries with your words, with your actions, and sometimes with the help of other people. Boundaries help you to be clear about what you are for and*

against and what you will and won't tolerate in your relationships" (Townsend, 2011).

"It is for freedom that Christ set us free; Stand firm, therefore, and do let yourselves be burdened again by a yoke of slavery" (Galatians 5:1).

As I prepared one week to lead a group on Overcoming Anxiety and how NOT to remain stuck, I remained prayerful as I trusted God to guide me. I wanted to be able to present the information that the group (yes, that included me) needed in order to remain hopeful—to lay their burdens down to bring greater peace to their lives. I will not sugarcoat it—it is a minute-by-minute work in progress for me. I do not have it all together. With God, I have all I need to get it all together, but I still seek Him constantly, setting healthy boundaries to have healthier and happier relationships that God has ordained to be a part of my future.

"FINALLY, BROTHERS, WHATEVER IS TRUE, WHATEVER IS honorable, whatever is just, whatever is pure, whatever is lovely, whatever is commendable, if there is any excellence, if there is anything worthy of praise, think about these things" (Philippians 4:8 NIV).

What or who has control over your life? Your time? Your thoughts? Are there healthy limits in your life so that you feel safe and protected and not judged? Self-reflect and note those things that cause you unnecessary stress. Set healthy limits in your life. Spend time doing the things you enjoy. Don't neglect yourself.

BOUNTY

A generous gift; something freely provided. Or a sum paid for killing or capturing a person or animal as in *Dog the Bounty Hunter*. Let's get back to that later.

I love and appreciate my home, family, friends, church family and the support in prayers and fellowship that they give me. I am certainly blessed beyond measure by all of these gifts from God.

"Blessed is the man who remains steadfast under trial, for when he has stood the test he will receive the crown of life, which God has promised to those who love him" (James 1:12 ESV).

I am equally blessed in my career. I describe my job as an elementary school principal as "the most difficult job I've ever loved." It is very true. Unless you have spent time at an elementary school these days, you have no clue—never a dull moment. We really try to laugh as much as possible. Sometimes it's all you have . . . joy and laughter in spite of the situation. There's no way to describe how busy we are—feeling that we NEVER get everything done. This is year five of my tenure as a principal and we have certainly seen a lot of changes, even a name change to the school. Every year there has been growth in our community, parent engagement, and students. We even added fifth grade this year, which I was so happy about.

I pride myself on making decisions that are best for our students. There have been many times that parents, students, and even teachers have not agreed with my decisions. I have prayed and even revisited those decisions to make sure they were best. It has certainly been a learning experience, one I will never forget.

This year, we were gifted at our school by some very generous donors. Last year, Dr. Dirk Rainwater, a local physician purchased activity chairs and tables for grades two through four. Students are working together now, asking each other critical questions and collaborating. I felt it was important to have those same tables and chairs for our fifth-grade students, but due to budget constraints and repairs at the school, the district was unable to assist with these purchases. However, I was determined to find a way.

I contacted a few local businesses and received a donation from them for part of the purchase. I was sharing this venture of mine with a dear friend and just like that he also made a hefty contribution. With the generosity of Jonesboro State Bank, Dr. Rainwater, and my personal friend, Eddie Philley, tables and chairs were delivered. They are in place and students are using them now.

That type of kind-heartedness is so refreshing in a day and time where much of the news is usually negative. God is still at work in our communities, in my school, and in our lives. This bounty has blessed me, my students, and my teachers more than we could ever express. Thank you, thank you, thank you—from the bottom of our hearts! May God continue to richly bless you for your generosity!

JEANANNE OLDHAM

"Oh give thanks to the Lord, for he is good; for his steadfast love endures forever" (1 Chronicles 16:34 ESV)!

How can you bless others today with bounty or goodness? The best blessing will be what you receive by giving to others. The giving does not need to be financial. A smile, a hug and listening ear are all gifts that are needed and appreciated. What gifts are you giving to others?

BURDENS

I was once asked to lead a Life Group on "Overcoming Anxiety". Don't laugh! I told a dear friend that when I volunteered to lead this group, I was not experiencing that much anxiety in my life. But God prepares us to grow in a way that extends beyond what we can imagine. I continue to remind myself that God does not call the qualified, but He qualifies the called.

The week before I led the group for the first time was a really tough one; I won't lie. I was fasting for several things that consumed my time and thoughts—to pray over our church, community, and country. We had a thirty-minute prayer time each night; I attended Sunday through Thursday, but I was still struggling. I admit that I cried and prayed more than I have in a very long time.

Disappointment is hard. Life is not easy. The struggle is real. By Friday of that week, my blood pressure was up (175/95), and I was having pains in the middle of my back. I closed the door to my office (not done often), turned the lights off, and tried to work quietly to calm myself. After two hours, my blood pressure was still a little too high so I left work a few minutes early.

The reason for my stress? I had picked my burdens back up. I did not leave them where I had laid them. Matthew 11:28-30 tells us, "Come to me, all you who are weary and burdened, and I will give you rest. Take my yoke upon you and learn from me, for I am gentle and humble in heart, and you will find rest for your souls. For my yoke is easy and my burden is light."

I talked with a friend who helped me work through the overwhelming parts of my life. I prayed, sang praises and headed out to spend time with my grandsons to attend the football game back home. It was like a good dose of medicine altogether. Peace and joy poured over me.

I am a Pollyanna. I always try to believe the glass is half full. There are problems with being a Pollyanna though. When I see things working out in life in my favor, I am usually FULL SPEED ahead. Because of this, I learned the hard way, which is not necessarily how God works. Full speed may not be His timing or His purpose for your life. A problem with learning to wait has been brought to my attention. It is a constant work in progress. We live in an instantaneous society. I am not alone in wanting what I want, when I want it, and how I want it. However, as children of God we have to learn to lay our burdens down . . . and wait.

We must have faith that God knows what is best for our life. We must believe that He will walk us through the times we worry that things won't work out. They may not work out like WE want them to, but they will work out what's best for us.

It's time to lay down the anxiety, worry, stress, sadness, anger, grief, fear, and doubt. Lay your burdens down. Yes, lay them ALL down. Do not pick them back up. Leave them at the feet of Jesus. Find hope in reading His word, praying, and crying out to Him. Seek Him out, praise Him for all the blessings you have in your life. Use the verses below to speak His word over your life this week.

- Cast all your anxiety on Him because he cares for you (1 Peter 5:7).
- Look to the Lord and his strength; seek his face always (Psalm 105:4).
- Cast your cares on the Lord, and He will sustain you; He will never let the righteous fall (Psalm 55:22).
- Do not grieve, for the joy of the Lord is your strength (Nehemiah 8:10).
- I have told you these things, so that in me you may have peace. In this world, you will have trouble. But take heart! I have overcome the world. (John 16:33).
- Do you not know? Have you not heard? The Lord is the everlasting God, the Creator of the ends of the earth. He will not grow tired or weary, and his understanding no one can fathom. He gives strength to the weary and increases the power of the weak (Isaiah 40:28-29).

WHAT BURDENS DO YOU NEED TO LAY DOWN TODAY? LET HIM take them from you. He is more equipped than we are. Experience the peace that passes all understanding . . . only available from Jesus.

CALLING

A few months ago, I had a very real experience at our women's conference concerning a different type of call on my life and felt I would soon be entering a new chapter in my life. I had very real experiences of hearing My Father God's voice telling me that I am His "baby girl" and an encourager. At the time this happened, I was still using my devotion time each morning to write an inspirational message. As time passed, it became more about sharing some of my innermost feelings, no matter how raw or real, which has been a growth experience for me.

It touches me when people tell me how my writings speak to them or that they are facing similar situations. It is a discipline for me to begin each day giving honor and praise to Heavenly Father. Starting my day in fellowship with Him has changed me in many ways. I still stumble and fall but find hope and joy in knowing that He is a forgiving God over and over again—He loves us that much. Ephesians 4:12 says, "And their calling is to nurture and prepare all the holy believers to do their own works of ministry, and as they do this they will enlarge and build up the body of Christ."

One of my first experiences at South Parkway, also known as LifeChurch.LA was having Mrs. Jeanette, one of our altar workers, pray with me about whether or not to apply for the principal job that I now hold. I had never intentionally prayed for guidance before when applying for a leadership position. I asked that she pray that God would give me a sign if I should apply, and that He would lead and guide my decisions in life in a way that would bring Him honor and praise. I wanted to answer the call on my life.

As soon as she finished praying, a very real peace came over me. I felt God was telling me that this was the job He had been preparing me for all my life. I did study and prepare before I applied and interviewed. Then it happened, I received the callback and was offered the job. It was only fitting that the call came while I was attending the church conference lunch. It was definitely a turning point in my life. It was confirmation that whatever we ask believing, we will receive.

Additionally, I received another confirmation at the women's conference two years later. I attended the Friday night and Saturday day sessions, but missed the evening service. On Sunday, I went to say goodbye to Chris and Erica Estrada, the speakers of the conference. In my visit with Erica, I shared that I was an elementary school principal and that I was eating lunch with Chris when I was offered the job years prior. She said, "I had a word for a principal last night, but I did not share it." I told her I had not been in attendance the night before. She said, "Here's the word for you. God says you are exactly where He has intended for you to be—stay the course."

Wow! It blew me away—confirmation that I was serving in the mission field that God had chosen for my purpose.

In Luke 22:26 TPT, it says, "But this is not your calling.

You will lead by a different model. The greatest one among you will live as one called to serve others without honor. The greatest honor and authority is reserved for the one who has a servant heart."

Notice that even after I experienced peace about applying, I still studied, researched, and prepared. That's the way a calling on our lives happens. It is not the waving of a wand—preparation is required. Preparation is required in anything worth having—a skill or talent, a friendship, a home, a marriage, a church, a family. It's been said, "Anything worth having is worth working for." As I wait on the Lord to reveal more about my future serving Him, I am searching Him out, seeking Him out, and waiting on His timing and for revelation and direction for me.

"For God's call on our lives is not to a life of *compromise and* perversion but to a life surrounded in holiness" (1 Thessalonians 4:7).

GOD HAS A CALLING FOR EACH OF US. HE EQUIPS US WITH different talents and strengths. He grows us intentionally. Our callings are each specific to His plan for our lives. What is He calling you to do today? Have you begun to seek out His purpose for your life? Have you prayed for a sign or revelation so you can begin to prepare?

Seek Him out today!

CLEAN

Someone told me one day that I take more baths than anyone he knows. In my defense, I had been outside sweating profusely and did not want to be embarrassed or offensive with my body odor. I have always heard the expression, "Cleanliness is next to godliness." We have all smelled someone and wondered, *how can they not smell themselves?*

Each and every day we need to become clean before our Lord. Hebrews 10:22 reminds us that we come closer to God and approach him with an open heart, fully convinced by faith that nothing will keep us at a distance from him. For our hearts have been sprinkled with blood to remove impurity and we have been freed from an accusing conscience and now we are clean, unstained, and presentable to God inside and out!

Our sinful nature requires us to ask forgiveness for our sins every day. Think of the Lord's Prayer. We can and should use it as a guide for our daily prayer time with Him. It is so much more than just telling Him what we want or need. He already knows anyway!

I can't help but feel strongly about verses 23-25 in

Hebrews because of the message, which states what we as Christians are charged to do:

> *So now we must cling tightly to the hope that lives within us, knowing that God always keeps his promises! Discover creative ways to encourage others and to motivate them toward acts of compassion, doing beautiful works as expressions of love. This is not the time to pull away and neglect meeting together, as some have formed the habit of doing, because we need each other! In fact, we should come together even more frequently, eager to encourage and urge each other onward as we anticipate that day dawning (Hebrews 10:22-25).*

WHO OR WHAT ARE YOU CLINGING TO? WHO OR WHAT ARE you in fellowship with? Find friends that will support and lift you up in prayer.

COMPROMISE

The word compromise used as a noun means an agreement or a settlement of a dispute that is reached by each side making concessions. As a verb, compromise means to settle a dispute by mutual concession. We have all made compromises. Sometimes just to keep the peace. We may have made compromises when we shouldn't have. Knowing full well what the right decision is, we sometimes fall prey to our flesh. Why do we do that? In relationships, concessions or compromises must be made on both sides, but as for our Christian walk—that's another story.

Did you ever hear the story about the man who couldn't decide which side of the Civil War he was going to fight for? He wore Confederate pants, a Union shirt, and was shot at by both sides. That's the way compromise is for the compromiser—one who straddles the fence or tries to live in both worlds, not committing or choosing a side. Living in two worlds is a miserable place to be.

Church-goers may have tried this before. We go to church when we want to. I mean, we all want to go to heaven, but we sin and live a worldly life until we need someone to rescue us. Then we are all about turning to God. This brings to mind the C&Es (Christmas & Easter Christians). That is not God's perfect design for how we should walk out our faith. 2 Timothy 4:3-4 ESV reminds us, "For the time is coming when people will not endure sound teaching, but having itching ears they will accumulate for themselves teachers to suit their own passions, and will turn away from listening to the truth and wander off into myths."

This may require us to set ourselves apart from the world in certain areas or ways. Not to say we think we are above anyone or anything, but we must be cautious of what we expose ourselves to so that we don't become of this world more than we are of God.

I think of the saying, "Garbage in, garbage out." What we feed our minds is what we become. For me, I have to constantly feed on Praise and Worship, Christian teachings and His Word because the devil is after me. He wants to defeat me and make me believe who I am NOT. I rebuke the attack of the enemy as often as he comes against me.

In order to not compromise our beliefs, we must defend our faith. As believers, we must "see to it that no one takes you captive through hollow and deceptive philosophy, which depends on human tradition and the basic principles of this world rather than on Christ" (Colossians 2:8; see also Hebrews 3:12). We are also commanded to be "prepared to make a defense to anyone who asks you for a reason for the hope that is in you…" (1 Peter 3:15 ESV).

God expects us to uphold the values in His Word by living a life that is acceptable to Him. Our prayer should always be that others see Christ in us, no matter what we are facing. Our witness can inspire others to "come to their senses and escape the snare of the devil…" (2 Timothy 2:26 ESV).

"Watch and pray so that you will not fall into temptation. The spirit is willing, but the body is weak" (Matthew 26:41 TLB). Speak God's word aloud. Remember Psalm 110:11 says, "His words will I hide in my heart that I might not sin against God."

TAKE A STAND TODAY FOR GOOD, NOT EVIL. TAKE A STAND for kindness. Do not compromise your beliefs. What have you compromised in your life? How has that experience given you wisdom to make better decisions in the future?

CONFUSION

There seems to be so much confusion these days. Confusion about the truth—mostly in the media. That was my reason for watching hardly any television or cutting out news. I have been told previously that I am burying my head in the sand by doing that, but I choose to think of it a different way. I am being selective about what my brain has to process. I am a deep thinker and take things to heart quickly, so limiting what I spend my time thinking about is important.

Confusion can affect our work productivity; it can affect our happiness, thought process, and yes, it can even affect our health. The enemy is KING of confusion. He loves to stir up angst among God's people. It is his goal to keep us confused about who we are, what we can do, what God's plan for our life is, what we do each day, who we interact with—Satan is addicted to confusion and loves to spread it in our thoughts and lives. But God . . .

1 Corinthians 14:33 NKJV tells us, "For God is not *the author* of confusion but of peace, as in all the churches of the saints." We should also be aware of spirits that may come

against us that seem one way, but instead are not of the heavenly realm. We are reminded in 1 John 4:1 that, "Beloved, do not believe every spirit, but test the spirits to see whether they are from God, for many false prophets have gone out into the world."

In John 14:26 ESV it says, "But the Helper, the Holy Spirit, whom the Father will send in my name, he will teach you all things and bring to your remembrance all that I have said to you." We are to search out the truth in God's word and surrender ourselves to the Holy Spirit and its teachings. When we do, this the state of confusion we are in will dwindle away.

There are many things of this world that we will never understand here on earth. Those will have to wait until we see him face-to-face. We must continue to trust and obey until that time.

"Ask, and it will be given to you; seek, and you will find; knock, and it will be opened to you" (Matthew 7:7).

Tanaaz Chubb, author of *The Power of Positive Energy* and creator of ForeverConscious.com, wrote an article about four things you can do when you are confused. I like these suggestions but would like to put a Biblical twist on them. There is an upside to being confused. Yep, I said it. We cannot live on top of the mountain. If we never struggled, we would never grow. If we were always certain about our next step, would we search out and seek God and His plan for our life so adamantly?

Here are the four things Chubb suggests you do to overcome your confusion and find the joy with my Biblical twist added:

1. Accept where you are. I propose to accept who you are and that you are on the path that God has

designed for your life if you are yielding to Him. Psalm 57:2 NLT says, "I cry out to God Most High, to God who fulfills his purpose for me." Sometimes we may feel that we have been stuck for a while in the same place. Maybe that's because we haven't learned everything we need to learn to be able to move forward. Our lesson has yet to be learned.

2. Take a deep breath. I propose that we pray about the answer not the problem and trust God. "Come to me, all you who are weary and burdened, and I will give you rest. Take my yoke upon you and learn from me, for I am gentle and humble in heart, and you will find rest for your souls. For my yoke is easy and my burden is light" (Matthew 11:28-30 NIV).

3. Focus on what you know. Psalm 32:8 ESV says, "I will instruct you and teach you in the way you should go; I will counsel you with my eye upon you." Look up to the One that knows it all.

4. Be patient. That one is a challenge for me as I have admitted before. Wait on the Lord. Be at peace with His timing and His wisdom. Seek the word of God—the truth. Trust and obey His word. Keep the faith.

Romans 12:12 ESV tells us to "Rejoice in hope, be patient in tribulation, be constant in prayer." Isaiah 40:31 ESV reminds us, "But they who wait for the Lord shall renew their strength; they shall mount up with wings like eagles; they shall run and not be weary; they shall walk and not faint."

FAITH WILL FIND YOU

Don't be confused about what is lasting in this life. Jesus Christ is our only and best hope during our times of suffering. How are you remaining grounded in Christ's teachings? Are you reading His word? Are you giving thanks, praying, and worshiping every day? If not, give it a try. It will truly make a difference in the quality of your daily life.

Depression Is a Spirit

Mental turmoil is defined as confusion, agitation, disquiet, is usually caused by emotional buildup (things never let go of), and usually brings fear. Fear does not come from God. 2 Tim. 1:7: "For God has not given us a spirit of fear, but of power and of love and of a sound mind."

The more we thank Him, the less we will be in self pity or murmuring, and we must kill all self pity, if we want to escape any oppression. Circumstances go up and down, but in everything we must give thanks.

"In everything give thanks, for this is the will of God in Christ Jesus concerning you" (1 Thess. 5:18). As Christians, we sometimes have a very tough time doing this, but this is the Bible's way of getting free from depression, getting the dark clouds to roll away and the sun to shine on our lives again. "So put on the garment of praise for the spirit of heaviness" (Isaiah 61).

Pastor Pat Buckley suggests we pray this prayer every time the heaviness comes on: "Thank you Father, I have the authority from the finished work of your Son. I rebuke this spirit of Heaviness; I command it to leave me, in the name of Jesus. I bind this spirit and command it to lose from me, I resist this heaviness and because I am submitted to God, it must and it will Flee" (James 4:7).

FOR THOSE WHO ARE FIGHTING THE SPIRIT OF DEPRESSION, rebuke it from your lives, your home, your family! Get into the presence of the Lord. Get out among others—push yourselves, if at all possible. Sometimes a change of scenery can make all the difference in the world. Get up and get ready to be in the presence of God today. Ask, "God, what are you saying to me today?" Rebuke any doubt or sadness. Do for others what you wish would be done for you. It will surely bless you!

Cemetery Beach, Grand Cayman Island, June 2019

CONVICTION

Sometimes harsh words can cause us to question how we are living. As humans, the flesh is our natural mode of operation. However, once we are saved and walking and talking with Jesus, we have the Holy Spirit to help us operate in the supernatural. As some say, He puts the super on our natural.

When we are seeking Him out, He will use people with pure intentions to help convict us of our wrongdoing. The enemy, however, will try to use the impure intentions of others to defeat us, break our spirit, or slow our momentum. But God can use that to help us go deeper within, to question how we can walk closer to Him. Our actions speak louder than our words. Right!?! How we treat others and what we do becomes who we are more than our written or spoken words.

Words of encouragement are inspiring, and even constructive criticism has given me reason to think more deeply about my life and EVERYTHING I do. Thank you for all of it!

"So stop being critical and condemning of other believers, but instead, determine to never deliberately cause a brother or sister to stumble and fall because of your actions. I am convinced by personal revelation from the Lord Jesus that there is nothing wrong with eating any food. But to the one who considers it to be unclean, it is unacceptable. If your brother or sister is offended because you insist on eating what you want, it is no longer love that rules your conduct. Why would you wound someone for whom the Messiah gave his life just so you can eat what you want?

Don't give people the opportunity to slander what you know to be good.

For the kingdom of God is not a matter of rules about food and drink, but is in the realm of the Holy Spirit, filled with righteousness, peace, and joy. Serving the Anointed One by walking in these kingdom realities pleases God and earns the respect of others. So then, make it your top priority to live a life of peace with harmony in your relationships, eagerly seeking to strengthen and encourage one another" (Romans 14:13-19).

Sometimes I get so involved in doing what I want that I forget how it might affect others around me. Jesus, help me to walk a path that is honorable to you. I don't know about you, but this is a work in progress for me. Jesus, help me walk this out.

WHAT WORK IS GOD DOING IN YOUR LIFE? WHAT ARE YOUR goals to be able to live out His purpose in your life? You are here for a reason. God wants to use you.

COVERING

I was getting ready to get away for a few days in the mountains when I realized my best bet for a jacket was Daddy's hunting coat (I hadn't worn it much in the past five years). I found it on the back seat of his truck after he passed away and decided to keep it.

When someone we love passes away, we yearn for ways to feel the closeness that we miss. Some go to the burial site. Some sit in their chair. We want something that belonged to them close to us. We may find comfort in wearing a piece of their clothing or sleeping on their pillow. Looking at pictures of all the memories that we made brings tears along with smiles and some laughter.

I found much comfort in the Montana mountains when I traveled there one fall recently. The scenery and peaceful atmosphere were healing. The covering of Daddy's coat was a different kind of comfort. Yes, I still yearn for his closeness, his advice, his laughter, and his big hugs. Wearing his coat and remembering the good times is a reminder that his closeness is forever near. He lives on in everyone he knew. He lives on in what he taught us . . . through his actions, not just his words.

We have physical coverings to keep us warm—blankets, quilts, coats, sweaters, socks, and caps. We also have emotional coverings—smiles through the pain, and laughter through the rain. Spiritually, Christ is our true covering. My favorite verse reminds me of how Jesus wraps His love around us.

"His massive arms are wrapped around you, protecting you. You can run under his covering of majesty and hide. His arms of faithfulness are a shield keeping you from harm" (Psalm 91:4).

WHAT ARE YOU COVERING UP TODAY? ARE YOU HURTING? Are you sad? Are you depressed? Reach out for help. Read His Holy Word. Get connected with a group that can help you through dark times.

In this picture my Daddy's jacket is covering a broken wrist. The smile on my face was covering the pain. Yellowstone National Park (2018)

CRAVINGS

Cravings can be defined as an intense, urgent, or abnormal desire or longing such as a craving for chocolate or a craving for new experiences. We've all had food cravings for dumplings or spaghetti, a Dr. Pepper or sweet tea, or whatever wets your whistle. Although our basic cravings are for thirst and hunger, there are more cravings to consider, which can satisfy and make us feel complete.

We crave love and affection. We crave friendship and companionship. We crave the ability to be healthy, wealthy, and wise. All of these are normal desires, but if we crave them more than we do the love and affection of our Father, they become idols. We should yearn for Him and be satisfied that He is enough.

I love Psalm 34:8 ESV, "Oh, taste and see that the LORD is good! Blessed is the man who takes refuge in him!" There is nothing as sweet as the goodness and mercy of the Lord.

There are triggers for our cravings. Just as an addict must figure out their triggers to avoid their addiction, we need to figure out our craving triggers. For example, carbohydrates make me crave sugar and vice versa. If we are not aware of these triggers, we may slip back into craving things that are not part of our changed lifestyle and eternal purpose.

All the more reason to stay in God's word and in prayer and surround yourself with fellow Christians who lift you up. A godly friendship is priceless. We have all had those friends that, as long as our association is beneficial to them, we are good, but the moment that the friendship is no longer beneficial, they are nowhere to be found. However, the more you surround yourself with friends running after God, you won't be disappointed. They will pray for you, with you, and over you. They hold your hand, cry with you, and continue to lift you up even when you don't know it.

One song that talks about craving Jesus even through difficulties is "Jesus, Bring the Rain," by MercyMe. When we truly crave God and desire His purpose on our life, we can say/sing this with our whole heart:

> *Bring me anything that brings You glory*
> *And I know there'll be days*
> *When this life brings me pain*
> *But if that's what it takes to praise You,*
> *Jesus, bring the rain*

What He brings us, even in the dark or rainy times, is what we need to draw nearer to Him, to crave the intimacy with Him. He is greater than anything we face. What is gained far outweighs our worldly cravings. "Do not love this world nor the things it offers you . . . for the world offers only a craving for physical pleasure, a craving for everything we see, and pride in our achievements and possessions. These are not from the Father but are from this world" (1 John 2:15-16 NLT).

FAITH WILL FIND YOU

WHAT ARE THE CRAVINGS THAT YOU DESIRE? IS A WALK WITH Jesus at the top of your priority list? Has the world overtaken your life? Is there room in your life for Him?

Don't miss the chance to make that change. Don't compromise what should be most important for things that will fade away quickly.

DIRECTION

If you know me well, you know I am a bit directionally challenged. It is something that is a constant work in progress. If I don't know the row number I park in at Walmart, I may spend a few minutes trying to locate my car when I come out, depending on how long I shopped. It's not a bad thing unless it is pouring down rain. Right?!?

As I look at my life, it seems it has been somewhat directionally challenged. I have experienced several missteps because of the direction I went with my life—bad decision making on my part, trying to do things "my way." So one day I heard Jesus say, "How's that working out for you, Jeananne?" And I knew it was time for a change. Thankfully, Jesus welcomes us all back in the fold like the prodigal son. He pursues us and leaves the ninety-nine to search us out, to rescue us from what life deals us but most commonly to rescue us from ourselves.

The direction of our walk with Him is one that, if we want to be intimate, requires us to search Him out to make sure we are following the path He has designed for us. He has a path and a plan for each of us—never doubt that!

Philippians 3:14 tells us to "...press on toward the goal to win the [heavenly] prize of the upward call of God in Christ Jesus." How do we do that? Well, Proverbs 3:5 TPT says to, "Trust in the Lord completely, and do not rely on your own opinions. With all your heart rely on him to guide you, and he will lead you in every decision you make."

Psalm 32:8 says it best: "I hear the Lord saying, 'I will stay close to you, instructing and guiding you along the pathway for your life. I will advise you along the way and lead you forth with my eyes as your guide. So don't make it difficult; don't be stubborn when I take you where you've not been before. Don't make me tug you and pull you along. Just come with me!'"

Sometimes we may want to crawl in a hole and hide away because things are not going well—work, career, relationships—they all give us challenges UNLESS we give our hearts and minds over to Him to give us encouragement and take His hand to walk us through. We must also study His word and spend time with Him in prayer. I find I have to do it alone, not only in church or on Wednesday nights. Try it if you haven't before.

When you feel like hiding away, turn to Him. He is our ultimate resting place. Picture this in your mind—His massive arms are wrapped around you, protecting you. You can run under his covering of majesty and hide. His arms of faithfulness are a shield keeping you from harm.

"Let Him be your compass and guide every day" (Psalm 91:4).

JEANANNE OLDHAM

DID YOU REALIZE THAT YOU CAN HIDE IN JESUS? HE IS OUR protector. Wrap yourself in His love. His word. His forgiveness. His peace today. Let Him recalculate your route in life.

EMPATHY

The capacity to feel another person's feelings, thoughts, or attitudes vicariously. Peter counseled Christians to have "compassion for one another; love as brothers, be tenderhearted, be courteous" (1 Peter 3:8, NKJV). The apostle Paul also encouraged empathy when he exhorted fellow Christians to "rejoice with those who rejoice; mourn with those who mourn" (Romans 12:15).

Empathy is related to sympathy but is narrower in focus and generally considered more deeply personal. As Pastor Dallas of LifeChurch.LA of Ruston Louisiana pointed out, the shortest verse in the Bible is also one of the most profound: Jesus wept. He was so touched and empathetic that he cried with Mary and Martha over their grief.

Compassion, sympathy, and empathy all have to do with the passion you have for another person's suffering. True empathy is the feeling of actually being a part of that suffering alongside them. All through the Bible, Jesus was empathetic, even being moved to raise people from the dead because of his compassion for others' pain.

It has always touched me when people show that kind of

sympathy for me. Maybe they attend a visitation of a loved one or they reach out and check on me. I have friends who pray over me whether I ask for it or not. When we receive empathy, it tends to help us be able to pay that kindness forward to others. I have been blessed with wonderful life-long friends—some are more recent than others but I am all the more thankful that God continues to bring Christian people into my life. Sometimes I feel my heart hurt for others when they are facing something. I don't even have to know what it is, but the Lord gives me a burden for them. That is what we do when we truly care and love others—we empathize with them. We suffer alongside them.

He cares for us and we need to remember that He hurts when we hurt. He feels the pain of His people. "You keep track of all my sorrows. You have collected all my tears in your bottle. You have recorded each one in your book" (Psalm 56:8, NLT). How comforting it is to know that God records all our tears and all our struggles! How good to remember God's invitation to cast all our cares upon Him, "because he cares for you" (1 Peter 5:7)! It goes back to treating others as we would want to be treated. Try kindness. Try empathy. Try compassion. Look around you. People are hurting everywhere. Reach out. It will certainly bless you when you do. Something amazing happens when you encourage or support others when you are struggling yourself. God will bless you. Give it a try!

IN YOUR TIMES OF SUFFERING, WHO REACHED OUT TO YOU? Maybe you need to reach out to someone today. Check on your friends. How can you be a better friend to others?

ENOUGH

Unfortunately, many of us have felt or been abandoned, forsaken or whatever you want to call it. It leaves us feeling insecure or undeserving. The devil uses our feelings of insecurity to gain a foothold on making us feel unworthy to be loved. Some children have been abandoned by a parent either physically or emotionally. Spouses or significant others have been abandoned sometimes when they least expected it, while some saw it coming but could not prevent the inevitable. The media portrays coupledom as the only way to go. How many times have you ever seen a movie that has a happy ending where someone was living a full and exciting life alone? NEVER! Failed relationships of all kinds leave us feeling as if we are simply not enough. The topic for this entry was originally "abandoned." However, after much prayer and some revelation, it was changed to enough.

We preach of finding joy unspeakable in our faith and our relationship with God being "enough," but inside most of us have a desire to be happily joined with a mate. One missing strand in many unions is that center, Jesus Christ. Many try to find happiness in others. If you are not happy within, you won't find your happiness in another person. Joy comes from within. Peace and contentment come from within. Without Christ as your cornerstone, the foundation of your relationship will crumble. There will be nothing that you can do to repair the damage. Building your home and heart on Jesus Christ is the only way to true happiness. The world may leave you feeling empty or abandoned or not enough. Friends or family may not always fill the void, but the one true answer is Jesus. He is always enough.

Deuteronomy 31:8 AMP tells us, "It is the Lord who goes before you; He will be with you. He will not fail you or abandon you. Do not fear or be dismayed." We strive for balance in our lives. Most of us miss the boat though—striving for that inner peace before we come into fellowship with others. We sometimes change who we are based on those we spend time with. That can be good when we surround ourselves with Christ-seeking friends. However, we must be cautious when our circle is a different clientele.

Following Christ does not exclude us from hurt, disappointment, or rejection in our life. That is not promised. What Jesus himself promised in Matthew 11:28-29 is, "Come to me, all of you who are weary and carry heavy burdens, and I will give you rest. Take my yoke upon you. Let me teach you, because I am humble and gentle at heart, and you will find rest for your souls."

We spend much more time with our coworkers and close friends than we do many of our family members. Most of us have been a part of a step or blended family before. We are either an in-law or maybe an outlaw. Some of are lucky enough to have friends who stick closer than a brother.

Our family speaks at each and every funeral about how we will NOT let so much time pass—that we will see each other before another loved one passes on. But most of the time, we fail at making that happen. Why? Because it is not a priority. We are so busy these days with other things—making a living, running kids to practices, attending family and church events, maybe volunteering. We say things many times out of emotion and then don't attach any action to make them happen.

Remember the old saying, "Actions speak louder than words?" It is so true. Words sound nice, but what really gives us the warm fuzzies is when someone DOES something that shows that they truly care for us. They remember our birthday or just call to check on us when a storm is passing through. They send us a text or even give us a token to show they appreciate us.

Proverbs 17:17 says," A dear friend will love you no matter what, and a family sticks together through all kinds of trouble." Unfortunately, most of us have experienced disappointment from friendships also. Psalm 55:20 says, "I was betrayed by my friend, though I lived in peace with him. While he was stretching out his hand of friendship, he was secretly breaking every promise he had ever made to me!" However there is one who is our promise keeper. And being a part of that family is most important. I loved the old Bill and Gloria Gaither song, "Family of God."

I'm so glad I'm a part of the Family of God,
I've been washed in the fountain, cleansed by His blood!
Joint heirs with Jesus as we travel this sod,
For I'm part of the family, The Family of God.

How do we know we are a part of the Family of God?

Romans 8:15 tells us, "For you did not receive the spirit of slavery to fall back into fear, but you have received the

Spirit of adoption as sons, by whom we cry, 'Abba! Father!'"

We are no longer orphans in Christ!

We are enough. You are enough. More than enough! Never doubt that. You may not be to some, but to God you are His precious child.

"God decided in advance to adopt us into his own family by bringing us to himself through Jesus Christ. This is what he wanted to do, and it gave him great pleasure" (Ephesians 1:5, NLT).

Whose family are you are part of? Where do you spend most of your time? What changes do you need to make in your life to be able to believe and live as if you are enough?

Life Church at Sunset

FAITH

The word faith has two definitions. One is complete trust or confidence in someone or something. Synonyms are trust, belief, or confidence. The second definition is a strong belief in God or in the doctrines of a religion, based on spiritual apprehension rather than proof. Synonyms for this are religion, church, ideology, belief, or teaching.

We trust or have faith in those people we have a track record with, correct? We have had people we trust until we don't because they give us a reason not to. That's our human nature. Sometimes our past leaves us with baggage that causes us to mistrust past experiences. It has nothing to do with the present situation.

With God, it is different because we have no reason to believe He will ever let us down. I take issue to a certain extent with the definition of faith being a strong belief in God based on spiritual apprehension rather than proof because we do have proof of what God can do, in a book we all know and love called the BIBLE. We have further proof if we will look back at other times in our lives. Take a look back to where you were and what you were going through a year ago. How about two or three years ago? Or even longer? I know my life has changed over the years and God has brought me through many things that I would have never survived on my own. God's mercy and grace carried me through.

2 Corinthians 5:7 tells us that we live by faith and not by sight. Is it easy? Well, no. Remember the saying, "Anything worth having is worth working for." It's that way in everything—our career, our family, our relationships. Nothing is just given with no work required. Romans 1 reminds us that when we come against the natural, think of the invisible. That is faith. Believing, praying, and having faith that your thoughts and actions come into alignment with God's will for your life. Another saying is that sometimes your reputation precedes you. That can be good or bad for us as humans, but with God it is only good.

Do you have faith that God is opening and closing doors for you? How can you strengthen your faith in God and trust Him more?

FEAR

"I will say of the Lord, 'He is my refuge and my fortress'" (Psalm 91;2 NLV). Fortress is a word we don't use much in our daily conversation. It means a strong, high place. The Passion Translation says it like this, "For you are my high fortress, where I'm kept safe. You are to me a stronghold of salvation. When you deliver me out of this peril, it will bring glory to your name. As you guide me forth I'll be kept safe from the hidden snares of the enemy—the secret traps that lie before me—for you have become my rock of strength."

Lysa TerKeurst does a great job dissecting Psalm 91. Here's my take away. God, being who He is, lifts us up above our earthly woes—fear, the spirit of defeat, bitterness, anger, and disappointment. That is how He is our fortress. We are lifted above our fear. Once lifted above, fear can't catch what it can't reach. We are far above our struggles when we are held safe in Him. To arrive in that safe place, we need prayer, we need worship, we need praise. To receive His protection daily, we need to commune with Him daily. It is truly a daily walk and talk. It is a choice we make every day.

JEANANNE OLDHAM

Fear is something that the enemy brings against us to put doubt into our hearts and minds about what God is willing and able to do in our lives. It affects our decisions, moods, and attitudes. Reading, writing, singing, and speaking His word is one way to help these truths become part of our thought process. All of them cement the words that should consume our minds—peace, joy, happiness, contentment, and faith. We need to practice faith instead of fear. As we reflect on the past and begin to plan for the future, let us never forget to pray, have faith, and believe. No fear, no doubt—let it go. Give it to God and move forward. Speak it into existence!

WHAT DO YOU FEAR? WHY DO YOU EXPERIENCE FEAR IN THAT part of your life? What is the root of that fear? Speak truth into your life daily to combat any fear or doubt that the enemy brings against you.

FRIENDSHIP

A godly friendship is priceless. Many people only show loyalty when something benefits them, but this should not be. We are not to act like the world. We are to respect others and show the love of Christ. We are not to manipulate others or put them down. We are to put others before ourselves. We are to conform our lives into the image of Christ. Not condemn.

Proverbs 17:17 NKJV says, "A friend loves at all times, and a brother is born for adversity."

We have all heard the saying, "With friends like this, who needs enemies." How we treat everyone matters, but especially those for whom we claim to care deeply and label them as our friend. We have friends from different areas of our life —childhood friends, school friends, hometown friends, church and/or work friends, party friends, and yes, even Facebook friends.

Just as quickly as new or long-lost friends enter or re-enter our lives, so too they sometimes exit quickly. Sometimes they relocate or you begin to run in different circles or the friendship just plays out. Sometimes they pass away. Do you ever wonder why people come and go in your life like a revolving door? We are creatures of habit. We get used to talking to and/or texting the same people, spending time with them, or reading and responding to their social posts, etc.

I have made efforts to surround myself with positive people. I don't need the drama or negativity or division that much of this world offers. That effort has extended to those friends I have on social media. I have been blessed to come back into fellowship with some I knew long ago.

I have a desire, and I believe a calling, to be an author, to inspire and encourage others. However, there is a misperception about people like me. People who like to reassure others who need encouragement and support, too. Just as other teachers need other teachers to network and receive support, so do principals, nurses, doctors, secretaries, receptionists, pipeliners, accountants, public servants, businesspeople, etc. We need contact with those who do what we do. We don't get that every day, but at some point in our life, we need it.

I had two fellow authors exit my writing world. So, my question to God was," Why God? What are you saying? What are you doing? I have lots of other friends who encourage me and support me, but writers need to learn from and rub shoulders with other writers. I have been blessed to be back in touch with one friend who is about to be published soon. Thank you, Leisa Spann, for sharing your writings with me and encouraging me.

I have been greatly saddened by the recent passing of my friend, Billy R. Philley. He wrote a daily "Coffee and Prayers" post on Facebook. It is what I read every morning. Several times for six months, he and I wrote on the same topic on the same day. We had a discussion about how that was the Holy Spirit. We both admitted that we were writing our posts the night before in Word and then copying and pasting the next morning in preparation for the books we were writing. We have prayed for one another several times and knew we could depend on each other as Christian friends. I will miss the interactions we had, those encouraging words from a fellow writer and friend.

As I have been in prayer and deep thought about the path my life has taken and is taking, God gave me the word, "Always." Yes, we have friends—maybe significant others, husbands, wives, best friends, coworkers, prayer warrior friends—but there are times we need someone and they are busy. There is only ONE friend who is ALWAYS here for us —God, Jesus Christ, the Holy Spirit—always faithful, always present, never absent, always listening, always caring, always loving us in spite of ourselves. He is saying to me, "You can ALWAYS depend on Me. Learn to talk and listen to Me, Jeananne. Hear what I say! I am leading and guiding you, minute by minute, hour by hour, day by day."

Hebrews 13:5 tells us that he will never fail us or abandon us. We need to let that soak in and take comfort that we are NEVER alone.

Is Christ leading and guiding your life these days? Do you depend on Him when you need a friend? What we need to do is simply reach out and talk with Him just as we do with our earthly friends. I know it is easier said than done sometimes. If you haven't, try it today. He is there. Ever present.

FUTURE

When we were growing up, we dreamed of a future that may have included a white picket fence and the perfect life. Some may have experienced the perfect life, or so it seemed until that dream faded away. Few of us were able to see that dream of our future come true. Why not? The choices we made did not give us those results. There are consequences to decisions.

Another problem is that we did not align our dreams with God's will for our life. He is the architect of our future. He IS the man with the plan. Fortune tellers or soothsayers may make predictions of our life, but God has a specific plan for all our tomorrows. If you are like me, a daydreamer, you have mapped out your future by visualizing what it would be like. But we must be reminded of Proverbs 16:9, "The heart of man plans his way, but the Lord establishes his steps." You see, He knows what's best for us.

From Perry Stone's book, *How to Interpret Dreams & Visions:*

The revelation the Holy Spirit brings forth involves

situations occurring now or in the future. At times you enter a season where you are uncertain of the will of God or of how to handle a difficult circumstance. Wisdom can be given by a revelation through the gift of the word of wisdom or the word of knowledge (1 Corinthians 12:8). We must never forget the revelation of our future is found through fellowship with the Holy Spirit. Our human nature cannot know of these things without intercession of the Holy Spirit. Jeremiah 29:11 tells us that Christ knows the plans and thoughts that He has for us, plans for peace and well-being and not for disaster, to give us future and a hope. The hope of our future is NOT found in horoscopes or storytellers, it is found in Jesus Christ.

In Matthew 7:7 we are reminded to, "Ask, and it will be given to you; seek, and you will find; knock, and it will be opened to you." He wants the best for us as long as it is aligned with His will for our lives.

Where is your hope found? What are your hopes and dreams for the future? Have you had a talk with God about them? Surrender to the Holy Spirit as God works in your life.

GLORY

According to God's word in Matthew 21:22 ESV we are reminded, "And whatever you ask in prayer, you will receive, if you have faith." Certainly, I am not proclaiming that we can selfishly ask for anything without giving God the honor and glory for his provisions, but I am a believer who claims visions and dreams that will grow His kingdom.

I made claim believing that I would have my book published in 2019. I began to organize it alphabetically (of course) in a Word document. The Lord began to drop a word into my heart to write about earlier this year. There were times when I felt God was giving me more than one word at once to write about, so I would jot them down to write about later. He always gives me my writings from scripture or stories or books I am reading at the time.

I generally have about two or more books that I am reading at once. I am a fan of both Bevere authors, Lisa and John. One morning I felt led to read from my John Bevere book, *Killing Kryptonite*. I had one topic that was unfinished in my book that perplexed me: Glory.

It's a word I personally don't use much. John's chapter on motivation speaks to us as a community of believers in this time of "darkness." He references 2 Timothy 4:3-4 that tells us a time will come when people won't listen to sound or wholesome teachings. They will be selfish and follow their hearts' earthly desires. They will turn their ears away from the truth. He also points out that during this time, authentic believers will stand out. They will shine! We should be stronger than the darkness.

What does that look like and how do we arrive? It will be such that even unbelievers will see His glory. Glory in Hebrew, "kabod," means splendor, greatness, wealth, might, abundance, honor, majesty, and heaviness. Every word up to the last one, we get. But heaviness? What does heaviness have to do with God's glory? It accentuates the fact that God operates at full strength in all of those—splendor, greatness, wealth, might, abundance, honor, and majesty (John Bevere, p.58).

Paul tells us in 2 Corinthians 4:6, that God has placed this knowledge "in our hearts so we could know the glory of God." He goes on to say that although we have this light shining in our hearts, we are like fragile clay jars containing great treasure. However, our great power is from God, it is not our own. We have the power to withstand through any darkness with God.

I also believe in signs and wonders, or as my friend, Leisa Spann calls them, "God Things." I do believe that as we strive to be more like Christ, He will bring deeper understanding about the things that perplex us. He guides my steps as much as I allow him to. I am adding the word "glory" to my everyday language.

JEANANNE OLDHAM

God's
Love
Overflows
Richly (on)
You

What "God Things" have you experienced in your life? Have you shared them with others? Why not? God's glory will be distributed when you give him the praise for what happens in your life.

GOD CARES

Recently, I have had a few friends who were struggling in their lives. I asked one, "Why are you are depressed?"

The reply was one I had not thought about before, "I don't know why I am depressed. Why would people think I know why?"

Once it was said, I realized how ridiculous my question was.

Our emotions can sometimes play tricks on us. Our minds are forever at work. I believe the devil plants negative thoughts in us. His goal is to kill, still, and destroy us. I like Lisa Bevere's take on this. She is a renowned Christian author and motivational speaker and wife of well-known author, John Bevere. She says to get an attitude with Satan. He attempts to distract, diminish, or divide. When those don't work, he moves to destroy.

So God has called me as an encourager. I am still learning how and what to say. It is a challenge for me. But one day, I opened my devotion, and it spoke to this very topic.

Psalm 31:18 tells us, "The Lord is close to the brokenhearted and saves those who are crushed in spirit."

Depression can be a result of losses from our present or past. It can come from the loss of hopes and dreams, even if you know the end of that dream has brought hope and goodness. Still, you grieve because that chapter of your life is over. It can come from experiencing personal loss of loved ones that you did not process at the time it happened. I know all too well about that.

Psalm is a great book to read when spiritual or emotional struggles come along. It is filled with cries to God for help, comfort, and strength. It reveals how much God cares about our pain and suffering. He stays close to us, showing His care and concern in many ways.

One blessing is to look around at the friends who provide you with encouragement and support. I know that I have been extremely blessed in this area. When those who are suffering from depression close themselves off, they lose perspective—they cut themselves off from how they really feel, or maybe they don't know how they really feel or why. It is so important to look at all the good in your life that God has provided to you. Thank Him for all the care He has afforded you. He cares for us.

Proverbs 18:24 reminds us, "Friends come and friends go, but a true friend sticks by you like family. God sends people into our lives by no accident." Other translations say, "closer than a brother."

I want to press upon you that there is no shame in seeking professional counseling.

Honestly, grief counseling with a Christian counselor put me on the path to where I am today. It literally saved my life and gave me hope to find my purpose. God is our refuge and strength, but He uses those around us in our time of need.

DON'T HIDE YOURSELF AWAY FROM OTHERS. BE REAL WITH what is going on in your life (and mind) with someone close to you. Remember, the one who loves us most, loves us best. He is never ashamed of where we are. Won't you move forward to find your peace today? Consider reaching out to someone else today.

Road tripping with my BFFs Spring Break 2019

GRACIOUS

The word today is gracious. A word mostly underused, except in the South. I grew up hearing and saying, "Goodness gracious alive…" And then there's the Jerry Lee Lewis song:

> You shake my nerves and you rattle my brain
> Too much love drives a man insane
> You broke my will, oh what a thrill
> Goodness gracious great balls of fire

Defined in the dictionary, it means courteous, kind, and pleasant. And then in Christian belief, it means showing divine grace. We have all experienced a gracious host. Thankfully, most all of us reading this have experienced the graciousness and mercy of our Father God. In Luke 10:27, we are directed to "love the Lord God with all your heart, all your passion, all your energy, and your every thought. And you must love your neighbor as well as you love yourself."

We are called to be gracious to others. We are called to treat people as Jesus would treat them if He were here on earth. When the Holy Spirit is within you, you recognize the needs of those around you and not your own needs (Dallas Witt). Psalm 57:3 states, "From heaven he will *send a father's help to* save me. He will trample down those who trample me. *Pause in his presence* He will always show me love by his gracious and constant care [italics added].".

In Acts 9, Saul was persecuting Christians and trying to have them thrown in prison. Because of his behavior, he was stricken blind. Ananias laid hands on him and Saul was healed and sighted again. He was immediately baptized. However, those he persecuted doubted he was a true disciple. Barnabas came to his defense, telling them how boldly Saul preached throughout the city in Jesus' mighty name.

Sometimes people doubt that we have really changed. They make judgments about who they think we really are. They see our actions and may hear our words, but they do not know our heart. The one and only gracious God knows our heart. He calls us His disciples. We have the ear to hear Jesus. He speaks to us in many ways—through our friends, music, in the beauty of nature around us, and the book He inspired for us, the Bible.

Psalm 112:4 tells us, "Even if darkness overtakes them, sunrise-brilliance will come bursting through because they are gracious to others, so tender and true." Following Jesus' example of being gracious is our calling as His children.

In Isaiah 45:3 it says, "I will give you the treasures of darkness [the hoarded treasures] And the hidden riches of secret places, So that you may know that it is I, The Lord, the God of Israel, who calls you (Cyrus the Great) by your name." We endure our trials so that we can support others when they face similar situations. Additionally, we are called to help others recognize their hidden treasures. Be the one that encourages others to run after what God is calling them to be. We are not called to be frightened of the darkness. We may feel ill-equipped, but that is a lie from the enemy. Be the Barnabas—gracious and kind. Our actions now affect our future generations.

"But Lord, your endless love stretches from one eternity to the other, unbroken and unrelenting toward those who fear you and those who bow facedown in awe before you. Your faithfulness to keep every gracious promise you've made passes from parents, to children, to grandchildren, and beyond" (Psalm 103:17).

Who are you encouraging and supporting others? Who is encouraging and supporting you? Give thanks for both today. Lift your friends up in prayer today.

GRATITUDE

I interviewed more than a dozen teacher candidates in the first five months of one year, hired six new teachers, and had all the slots filled—or so I thought—only to learn of more changes. And even after all of that, I still needed to do more interviews in order to be fully staffed. I enjoy interviewing teachers. It gives me a chance to see what they are about and if their hearts are open to love our Jonesboro-Hodge Elementary School children. You have to have a heart for teaching today with all the changes in curriculum and in the dynamics of homes life.

This is the first job I really prayed over before I applied. I do feel that it is my calling and my mission, and it has been an interesting and difficult journey at times. I have learned so much! And yet, I still have so much more to learn.

Something really touched me about a couple of the candidates I interviewed recently. In many ways they were quite different from one another. They had different levels of experience, taught different content and grade levels, and were even different genders, but they had one thing in common.

Neither been the recipient of gratitude in their previous jobs. They felt mostly that what they heard was negative. They had not been built up, but torn down. It made me sad for them. It caused me great reflection. Jesus, please help me have a heart of gratitude over my faculty and staff this year. Hopefully, I will be hiring both of these candidates and they will feel appreciated because of our attitudes of gratitude.

In Psalm 100:4 it says, "Enter His gates (presence) with a song of thanksgiving and His courts with praise. Be thankful to Him, bless and praise His name."

It is so important to thank those people around you who support and encourage you. It makes a difference in their heart and attitude, but it also makes a difference in ours.

I like the saying, "Sometimes we can't see the forest for the trees." People complain about their job but don't realize it is the reason they have their home, their ride, the food they eat. It's not that we don't all have some issues or struggles at work because we ALL do. It is so important to focus on what good we do have in our lives—look around you! We need to remember 1 Thessalonians 5: 18, "And in the midst of everything be always giving thanks, for this is God's perfect plan for you in Christ Jesus."

1 Thessalonians 5:18 verses 16–18 identifies three areas in our lives we must focus on: (1) unbounded joy; (2) praying continually; and (3) giving thanks to God no matter what happens in our lives. These three virtues combine to form the wonderful expression of Christ's life within us.

My prayer today is to have a heart of thanksgiving. Let me begin. Thank you to all my friends and family who have encouraged me to continue to share what God lays on my heart. He is working in my life because I opened the door. We all have gifts to use in His kingdom. If you don't know what

FAITH WILL FIND YOU

yours is, seek Him out. Enter into His presence today with a thankful heart. God is so so good! Amen!

WHAT IS YOUR PRAYER OF THANKSGIVING TODAY? HOW CAN you live a more grateful life? Every day give thanks for at least three things in your life. Begin the day this way and it will make a difference.

GRIEF

I remember the moment when my school, Jonesboro-Hodge Elementary, lost a former student, Billy Dewayne Adams. I remember the heavy heart I felt for his mother, Amy. The heavy heart I had for his brother and sisters, for our community of teachers and friends that all loved him. Grief can turn your world on a dime. It can bring darkness that you think you will never escape—IF you allow it. If we don't turn to our Heavenly Father for comfort and peace, it can destroy us.

Psalm 34:18 reminds us that the Lord is close to the brokenhearted and saves those who are crushed in spirit.

"God is our refuge and strength [mighty and impenetrable], A very present and well-proved help in trouble..." (Psalm 46:1 AMPC).

There is no shame in also reaching out for professional counseling. It made all the difference for me. Reach out to a friend or your pastor. Find a church home. Do something! Doing nothing will not bring about the change you need to get to the other side of what you are facing. Doing for others during this time is difficult but you will be blessed and it will give you an outlet and blessing to give back even when you don't feel like it.

"Be strong and courageous. Do not be afraid or terrified because of them, for the LORD your God goes with you; he will never leave you nor forsake you" (Deuteronomy 31:6).

THERE ARE SO MANY AROUND US HURTING AND SEARCHING for answers. Step out in Faith today and check on someone. If you have not processed grief or loss from your past, I encourage you to do that.

What losses are you holding on to? Are they making you bitter? If you are sad for an extended time, please reach out for help. There is no shame in that.

GROUNDED AND SANE

Today on this the Lord's day, I am reminded of what corporate worship and prayer does for me. It helps me remain grounded and sane. Those who know me intimately may disagree that I am grounded or sane! It is, however, my goal. The definition of grounded is someone or something stable, sincere, practical, or firmly established. An example of grounded is someone who reacts calmly in a crisis. I must admit I am better at times about reacting calmly in my professional life than in my personal life. There are times I still fail there also.

We all know what being sane means. We haven't been shipped off to the Looney Bin . . . yet. People's perception of sane is a funny thing. What we observe from the outside is not always the true picture of what goes on inside. It reminds me of "behind closed doors"—we never know how someone else is living behind the scenes.

God is the only one who truly knows our heart and our thoughts and intentions. Others can only perceive or think they understand us by our actions. It is important that our actions reflect the teachings of God. I know there are people who do not attend church regularly, and I am by no means judging, but for me, I know that I need every source of Jesus to be able to remain grounded in Him. And yes, I still fail. We are only human, but by the grace and mercy of God can we rise above our natural selves.

It is essential that daily we connect with God. Some pray, read scripture, and praise and worship at home, but there is an anointed power when we come together with other believers. One translation, The Christian Bible Standard, says it like this in Hebrews 10:25: "Not forsaking our own assembling together, as is the habit of some, but encouraging one another; and all the more as you see the day drawing near."

The Passion Translation says it like this, "This is not the time to pull away and neglect meeting together, as some have formed the habit of doing, because we need each other! In fact, we should come together even more frequently, eager to encourage and urge each other onward as we anticipate that day dawning."

All of this to say . . . Go to church to be in God's presence and with other believers every time you get a chance. This is what keeps me grounded (rooted) in Christ and sane (most of the time). I just have to do me how God leads. You do you, but make sure you are following the one who has the best of intentions for your life. I leave you with Ephesians 3:17, "Then, by constantly using your faith, the life of Christ will be released deep inside you, and the resting place of his love will become the very source and root of your life."

"For he will be [nourished] like a tree planted by the waters, that spreads out its roots by the river; And will not fear the heat when it comes; But its leaves will be green and moist. And it will not be anxious and concerned in a year of drought nor stop bearing fruit" (Jeremiah 17:8 AMP).

JEANANNE OLDHAM

God loves you. More than you can ever imagine! He wants to spend time with you! How will you honor Him? Are you connected at your church or is it just a checked mark off your list? Where are you plugged in?

HABIT

A habit is defined as a settled or regular tendency or practice, especially one that is hard to give up. We all have good habits and not so good habits. In order to make changes, we have to be intentional in what we do.

According to author James Clear, research says a habit is formed after sixty-six days. Some say it depends on the habit you are trying to get firmly in place. Dr. Maltz, a plastic surgeon from the 1950s, wrote about these experiences and said, "These, and many other commonly observed phenomena tend to show that it requires a minimum of about twenty-one days for an old mental image to dissolve and a new one to jell." Other research indicates that forming a new habit can take as little as eighteen days and as much as 254 days.

We have all had good and bad habits. Then there are those habits that are changed for you without your request or desire. People come in and out of our lives without permission from us. We get in the habit of talking to them daily or several times a day for a long while, maybe even years. Then one day, the phone calls and visits stop.

Change is not always easy. How you fill that void becomes a new habit.

This reminds me again of the saying, "Anything worth having is worth working for." Our Christian walk is like that. Our relationship with God and how much we fellowship is a good habit to form. Psalm 1:2 AMP tells us, "But his delight is in the law of the Lord, And on His law [His precepts and teachings] he [habitually] meditates day and night."

It may seem that some of us have it all together. Well, we don't. Looks are deceiving. The only one that truly know our habits, our thoughts, our heart is God. In Proverbs 5:21 it says, "For God sees everything you do and his eyes are wide open as he observes every single habit you have." Me, I am working on forming some new habits. I know what tendencies I have when I get down and out or become exhausted. What we tend to forget during these "struggle bus" times is how much we need each other.

Call each other, check on each other, get together. We are reminded of this in Hebrews 10:25, "This is not the time to pull away and neglect meeting together, as some have formed the habit of doing, because we need each other! In fact, we should come together even more frequently, eager to encourage and urge each other onward as we anticipate that day dawning."

WHAT NEW HABITS ARE NECESSARY FOR YOU TO MAKE? Don't struggle alone. Reach out. Become a part of a group that cares for you. Prays for you and lifts you up. Be a part of people that celebrate with you.

HATRED

September 11. It is so difficult to imagine that amount of hatred. I am still in awe that anyone could plan to take lives like they did that fatal day. It was a blow to our society. It was a blow to our nation and our world. It is still unimaginable, shocking, and horrific. God is our only hope in times like these. Today I pray for our country, our leaders, and the hearts and minds of all those who still struggle from the loss so great.

We lost so much that day. The sacrifice was tremendous. We are a nation of believers. May we have a coming together because of what we have been through and not forget to lift up one another up. Compassion and love, not hatred.

Father God please change hearts and minds. Align our thoughts with your will. Bless the United States of America and our leadership with love and wisdom to protect our country. May we never forget the sacrifices made for us. Thank you, Father, for yours. In Jesus name. Amen.

"If my people who are called by my name humble themselves and pray and seek my face and turn from their wicked ways, then I will hear from heaven and will forgive their sin and heal their land" (2 Chronicles 7:14).

EVEN AS JESUS HUNG SO CRUELLY ON THE CROSS, HE STILL showed mercy and asked God for forgiveness for his persecutors that murdered him. What mercy can you extend to those who persecute or treat you badly? This is a difficult task. Pray for those who seek to harm you.

HEARING GOD'S VOICE

Some may wonder what hearing God's voice means. It's not an audible voice like a ghost that we see in movies. It is the voice inside my head that prompts me to share matters of my heart. Over the past few months, I have been very transparent about parts of my life that before now I have not shared. Is it easy? No! And it is sometimes uncomfortable—but I feel led. I know that voice leading and guiding me is the Holy Spirit, and I know he uses me as a vessel to speak to others. I have been very blessed to be contacted privately and through Facebook several times over the past few months, PROOF that God uses us to bless, encourage, and support others who can relate.

Prayer, not always spoken aloud, is the communication between us and God. I have had prayers answered just from what I thought. I have many times said or thought, *God, I give you this situation, it is yours and no longer mine*, and quickly the phone rings or a text comes across my screen. HE DOES answer PRAYER!!!

JEANANNE OLDHAM

One day, a dear friend reached out to me with a need she had hidden for years. God brings people into our lives when we open ourselves to others. He blesses us for putting ourselves out there. He uses our past healing so we can bless others. He is so good. I am blessed beyond measure. Won't you let God use you to bless someone today, tomorrow, maybe every day? God will use you in a mighty way when you share with others.

HOME

Home sweet home. We all agree that it is near and dear to our hearts. I have lived in sixteen different homes or locations, including dorms at Northeast Louisiana University. I have lived in an apartment, a camp, camper, trailer house, and different types of conventional homes. Besides my home now, my fondest memories are of the duplex that we lived in when I was born. My great-grandmother, Grannie Oldham lived in the other side of the duplex. Maybe it's because I loved my Grannie so much and enjoyed spending time with her.

There are various things that can make you enjoy or appreciate your home. No matter the size, costs, or age of your home, there's one thing that is common—it's the place where you rest. It is predictable and secure. It is your stopping place at the end of a long, hard day. Your favorite chair awaits, your pet or mate greets you as you are ready to wind down.

One of my favorite songs about home is "Home Where I Belong" by B.J. Thomas. I used to play the piano and sing it at church back in Oak Grove. Home is such a comforting place. We have our house (home), but we also have our church home. And then there are those people with whom we have such a deep connection that we feel like we are home. We are so comfortable when we are with them that their presence becomes much like "a safe place."

Another favorite song of mine is "Feels Like Home," from the movie *Michael*, and sung by Bonnie Raitt. There's the ever popular, "Country Roads Take Me Home" that John Denver belts out. Lynrd Skynrd's "Sweet Home Alabama" is another song that most everyone knows.

The Bible is evidence that home has a physical and spiritual meaning. Physically, the Bible talks of building our houses on a firm foundation instead of on the sand. Hebrews 3:4 tells us, "For every house is built by someone, but God is the builder of everything." Isaiah 32:18 says, "My people will live in peaceful dwelling places, in secure homes, in undisturbed places of rest." John 14:1-2 remind us, "Do not let your hearts be troubled. You believe in God; believe also in me. My Father's house has many rooms; if that were not so, would I have told you that I am going there to prepare a place for you?"

The spiritual aspect of home is that our bodies are the temple of God. I Corinthians 6:19 asks, "Or do you not know that your body is a temple of the Holy Spirit who is in you, whom you have from God, and that you are not your own?"

For almost five years, I traveled and was away from home often. Although I enjoyed many aspects of that job, it was hard to be on the road so much traveling to different places. It was nice to be settled into a new home with a new job and not traveling so much. You've heard the saying, "Home is where the heart is." Of course, our literal heart is always with us, but what about our love. Where is it? Similarly, when people ask you where you are from, do you say the place you now live?

Not me, I am always from Oak Grove or West Carroll Parish. I have not lived there since 1991, but it is always home.

We live in a house. We call it a home. The spirit of God lives within us. As His temple what kind of housing are we providing? Most of us can quote that all familiar verse from Joshua 24:15, "As for me and my house, we will serve the Lord." What or who does your house serve?

HOSTAGE NO MORE!

No matter what we face, we know that our Father God, our Savior is there with us. He can take something that Satan means for harm and make it into something good. Much like taking lemons and making lemonade. We all think of things after the fact—like 20/20 vision.

If we are honest, we will think of things that happen that changed our path. At the time, it did not seem like a blessing, but in the long run it was. Sometimes things hold us hostage until something unfortunate happens. It may cause pain at the present time, but eventually we may see how much freedom comes after our release from that addiction, pain, grief, heartbreak—and we come out the other side stronger, joyous, pain-free. No longer a hostage!

Let me be clear, the Anointed One has set us free—not partially, but completely and wonderfully free! We must always cherish this truth and stubbornly refuse to go back into the bondage of our past (Galatians 5:1 TPT [*A Life of Freedom*]).

How we handle ourselves during the difficult times of our

lives matters. During those seasons, it is important we are absorbed in positive and constructive media and resources. Me—I love to read (books, the Bible, etc.) and listen to messages online in addition to my music, of course. This continues to resonate with me. A very special friend, Pat Hutson Bruner, supported me during a difficult time. Here's one message she shared with me:

The Word says that all things are held together in Christ Jesus. From that, I hear Him saying that for the Believer, it is actually impossible to fall apart (as the enemy tries to tell us we are doing), because any falling apart is done in the safety of His hands, the One Who holds us together. So, don't be afraid that the dam might break and be irreparable; because He holds us and will only deconstruct our lives in order to rebuild into something greater and better . . . for us and the Kingdom.

"Yet all of this was so that he would redeem and set free all those held hostage to the written law so that we would receive our freedom and a full legal adoption as his children" (Galatians 4:5).

TODAY, 87 PERCENT OF THE HUNDRED BILLION (PLUS) dollars spent on prescription drugs is spent on pain meds. Are we coping or celebrating? Are we enjoying our lives or do we ignore dealing with the pain? He can free us from whatever holds us captive. He is our chain-breaker, pain-taker, and dream-maker!

ISOLATION

One Sunday's message by Sister Paige Witt was so profound. The new series is titled, "Fully Known." She began by sharing that she has been known to say, "I can't let all this crazy out." We say things like that out of fear. Fear of what others would think of us. She went on to point out that most of us are "professional pretenders." We put on masks to hide what is going on behind the scenes, behind the smiles.

We are genius at camouflaging what we don't want others to see.

Covering up or isolating ourselves from Christ is not keeping us safe from God. We have to give Him access to all the failures in our lives, even in the midst of our struggles. Instead of clinging to Him in the middle of our mess, most of us retreat and go into failure mode, and then we allow ourselves to go into loneliness mode just because we don't want to face what our life is really like. We isolate ourselves.

From others. From church, maybe. From family and from friends.

The ironic thing about our actions is that we can't hide who we really are from God. He knows everything about us. Our failures, our fake smiles, our heartaches, our sour attitudes, our bitterness—He knows it ALL. Most importantly, Sister Paige reminded us that Jesus died for us as sinners, not as our forgiven, sanctified selves. First, we must give Him access to our heart and mind. Psalm 139: 1-6 expresses this:

> 1 O LORD, you have examined my heart
> and know everything about me.
> 2 You know when I sit down or stand up.
> You know my thoughts even when I'm far away.
> 3 You see me when I travel
> and when I rest at home.
> You know everything I do.
> 4 You know what I am going to say
> even before I say it, LORD.
> 5 You go before me and follow me.
> You place your hand of blessing on my head.
> 6 Such knowledge is too wonderful for me,
> too great for me to understand!

Next, we need to accept the vastness of His love for us. We find that in verses 13-17:

> 13 You made all the delicate, inner parts of my body
> and knit me together in my mother's womb.
> 14 Thank you for making me so wonderfully complex!
> Your workmanship is marvelous—how well I know it.
> 15 You watched me as I was being formed in utter

seclusion,
as I was woven together in the dark of the womb.
16 You saw me before I was born.
Every day of my life was recorded in your book.
Every moment was laid out
before a single day had passed.
17 How precious are your thoughts about me, O God.
They cannot be numbered!
Then we have to ask Him to come in and do a work
in us.
23 Search me, O God, and know my heart;
test me and know my anxious thoughts.
24 Point out anything in me that offends you,
and lead me along the path of everlasting life.

Sister Paige's story that Sunday of the woman at the well really hit home with me in the way that she interpreted it. Jesus pointed out that the woman at the well had five husbands previously and was living with a man who was not her husband. Most interpret that Jesus was calling her out for her sin, but another perspective is that Jesus knew the rejection she felt from those failed marriages. He knew her heart and her failures. That's why he offered her a drink of living water. He knew it was the only thing that would bring her complete healing.

Coming back into fellowship with my Savior brought and still brings healing for me. Being an active member of a church—serving, growing, being connected—brings me safety and security. There is safety in community; we feel safe in our neighborhood when we are surrounded by people we know and trust. People we can count on. Small groups and serve teams are a safe place just when we need it most.

I remember the very night sitting in *Girlfriends* at my

church (a women's group at LifeChurch.LA in Ruston, LA) a couple years ago when I realized it had been over twenty-five years since I had been a part of a church family. Tears poured down my face. They were tears of relief. Relief that the isolation I had lived in for so many years was over. The walls were broken down. I had allowed myself to connect with others. I had given Jesus access to my heart, mind, and life again. I invited Him to guide and direct my path. Although the road is still bumpy from time to time, I know He travels with me.

Serving will bring you out of a life of isolation or cover up. It takes our minds off of ourselves and changes our focus to others. If you are not a regular member of a serve team, try it out. I don't believe it will be a decision you will regret. Be blessed by serving.

How can you give back at your church and/or community? Will you step outside of your comfort zone and serve others in a way you never have before? You will definitely be blessed when you do.

Cemetery Beach, Grand Cayman Island, 2019

JUSTIFY

As of 2018, Justify is only the second horse to win the American Triple Crown with an undefeated record. Of the 13 American Triple Crown winners, Justify is the first who did not race as a two-year-old. He was initially sent to a trainer but pulled a muscle and was given time to recover and grow into his frame. His first win was when he was just shy of three years old. Justify grew into a large horse, standing 16.3 hands (67 inches) at the withers and weighing 1,380 pounds. A large horse who was light on his feet, for sure.

Adding some additional seasoning to the story of this brilliant animal is the jockey who made all kinds of news with his comments after the race. Mike Smith, the jockey riding Justify in the Belmont Stakes, could have said anything in his first television interview after the Derby win. Instead of thanking the horse's owner and trainer, Smith garnered extra attention by telling reporters, "I just want to thank my Lord and Savior Jesus Christ for blessing us on this afternoon and blessing us with this amazing horse." And still unashamed and very proud, he told CBN News in another interview how he prepares for a big race—with training strategy and prayer.

At the age of 52, Smith, a devout Christian, is the oldest jockey to win the Triple Crown to date. Justify broke the 136-year-old "curse of Apollo" by winning the Kentucky Derby without having raced at two years of age. The last time this feat was accomplished was by Apollo in the 1882 race. Mike Smith and Justify were an underdog team, two unlikely winners—an older jockey riding a very large racehorse who had suffered an injury and had not raced as a two-year-old uncommon. But then there's God. Smith boldly declared that it was prayer and a training strategy that put them on this winning path. So as Christians, what is our game plan or training strategy? Pray, read the Bible, attend and serve at a church, live out what the Word says.

Proverbs 14:12 tells us, "You can rationalize it all you want and justify the path of error you have chosen, but you'll find out in the end that you took the road to destruction."

Additionally, 2 Corinthians 12:19 says, "I hope that you don't assume that all this time we have simply been justifying ourselves in your eyes? Beloved ones, we have been speaking to you in the sight of God as those joined to Christ, and everything we do is meant to build you up and make you stronger in your faith."

Additional research about Mike Smith revealed that his parents divorced when he was a small child. He began riding races at eleven years old in his native home of New Mexico. He dropped out of high school his freshman year before receiving his jockey license at age sixteen in 1982. He married a jockey's daughter, but it ended in divorce. He has had over 33,000 mounts—over five thousand in first place and over eight thousand in second and third. He has earned over 314 million dollars in his career, although his winning percentage is less than 20%.

Smith's unlikely history (past) did not predict his future. This should speak to all of us! Think about it. The trials we face make us stronger. The failures we experience give us character. I believe Mike Smith will certainly continue to be blessed for his bold, public courage to give God honor and praise in the unlikeliest of places—the media. "I just couldn't keep it inside of me," Smith told CBN News. "I truly give God all the glory and I had to say it. Without Him, I wouldn't have all the success I do."

Smith said that when he's mounted on his horse, he follows God just as he normally would. "I believe there's just a flow that guides me and when I follow it, amazing things happen. And that's with everyday life, too. When God's leading you, you follow it."

Once the chains are loosed, we are set free. Our character does not change, but God changes our status. The blood that Jesus Christ shed gave the perfect sacrifice. His brokenness and death covers all of our sins, past, present, and future. We are then justified, even though we still fall short. Thankfully, our salvation is not dependent on our works. We are also the unlikely, the broken, the scarred, the frightened, the doubtful—but blessed, favored, righteous, redeemed, and yes, justified to be His child.

ARE WE UNASHAMED TO SHARE HOW OUR REDEEMER RESCUED us? We should NEVER be too proud to go public with our faith. How can you be bolder about what God has done in your life?

LEAN TIMES

Most of us can look back and remember a time when we were lacking financially, emotionally, spiritually or maybe even physically. Some of us may still be experiencing them from time to time. These deficiencies may have occurred at the same time. I have experienced them all at different points in my life.

The one that affected my life most negatively (or greatly) was the spiritual lacking that I experienced for years after being out of church or what we call out of fellowship with God. It does not mean that I did not love the Lord or that I did not believe in Him. It simply meant that I was not seeking Him out. I was not living out His purpose for my life on a daily basis. I was not listening for His Whisper.

Usually, there are instances that bring us back into fellowship. Sometimes they are tragic or sad events that give us pause, making us realize something has got to change. You realize your mode of operation has to change. Mine was the loss of my father. I literally fell to pieces when he passed. It turned my life on a dime, but God reminded me in Nehemiah

8:10 NIV, "Do not grieve, for the joy of the Lord is my strength." And my seeking began.

Find hope for yourself today in these verses from Psalm 46:

> *God, you're such a safe and powerful place to find refuge! You're a proven help in time of trouble—more than enough and always available whenever I need you. So we will never fear even if every structure of support were to crumble away. We will not fear even when the earth quakes and shakes, moving mountains and casting them into the sea. For the raging roar of stormy winds and crashing waves cannot erode our faith in you. Pause in his presence God has a constantly flowing river whose sparkling streams bring joy and delight to his people. His river flows right through the city of God Most High, into his holy dwelling places. Surrender your anxiety! Be silent and stop your striving and you will see that I am God. I am the God above all the nations, and I will be exalted throughout the whole earth. Here he stands! The Commander! The mighty Lord of Angel Armies is on our side! The God of Jacob fights for us! Pause in his presence (verses 1-4, 10-11).*

WHAT IS MISSING IN YOUR LIFE TODAY? DON'T LET IT KEEP you from making a change that can bring you through the other side of what you are facing. Allow yourself to be in His presence today. You will find peace there. You will find hope there. You will find his undeniable and indescribable love there.

LEMONADE

We've all heard the saying, "When life gives you lemons, make lemonade." I am sure that most everyone has felt like they have been dealt some lemons in their life. We even speak of an unreliable car being a "lemon."

I heard an older Phil Vassar song from 2009 the other day and thought, *Hey, man. I can relate to that.* Below are the lyrics to "Lemonade":

> *Sometimes you're the king, sometimes you rule*
> *Sometimes you're the joker man or playing the fool...*
> *But you've gotta play the game so why play it safe*
> *Life's about changes, lemons into lemonade.*

It may seem that some lemony situations leave such a sour taste that we find it difficult to move on. If we don't take it to God, it will leave a bitter taste in our mouths and may even harden our hearts. There are many ways people process their suffering—talking to a friend, writing about it, praying, praising, worshiping, and crying (there's that one, too).

Some situations may take all of these skills to help you walk through the pain. We should always turn to the word of God. It has scriptures to encourage and teach us in every situation. God did that for us on purpose—He inspired stories to which we can relate and gain perspective. No matter what we face, we should be reminded of the people in the Bible who faced adversity.

Certainly, Job suffered much but remained faithful. Satan specifically asked to test Job's faith and Job lost his children and all his worldly possessions. He lost it all to be tested. Job's friends and family tried to tell him that he must have sin in his life since he experienced so much hardship. They believed that if you are living faithfully, you will have success. Job understood this, but he still had to pass through the trials and tests.

I know that you can do all things, and that no purpose of yours can be thwarted. "Who is this that hides counsel without knowledge? Therefore I have uttered what I did not understand, things too wonderful for me, which I did not know" (Job 42:1–3).

Job was not God. No one knows more about what we need in our life than God does. He prunes us and corrects us, and yes, He uses hardships in our lives to grow us spiritually. He is there for us constantly. If at times He seems distant from us, it is not us who has moved.

During our times of trials and tribulations, we should push in closer to God. Lean more on Him, not less. We should also be reminded that no matter what we lose in this life, we can never lose our relationship with Jesus Christ. The book of Job ends with Job receiving even more wealth and possessions and children than he had at first. We can take heart knowing that the day will come when our own final restoration and renewal will take place in the new heavens and the new earth (Rev. 21:4).

I love this poem by Annie Johnson Flint that reminds us of what God has and has not promised.

"What God Has Promised"

God hath not promised skies always blue,
Flower–strewn pathways all our lives through;
God hath not promised sun without rain,
Joy without sorrow, peace without pain.
God hath not promised we shall not know
Toil and temptation, trouble and woe;
He hath not told us we shall not bear
Many a burden, many a care.
God hath not promised smooth roads and wide,
Swift, easy travel, needing no guide;
Never a mountain, rocky and steep,
Never a river, turbid and deep.
But God hath promised strength for the day,
Rest for the laborer, light for the way,
Grace for the trials, help from above,
Unfailing sympathy, undying love.

Find comfort today in these scriptures:

"Fear not, for I am with you; Be not dismayed, for I am your God. I will strengthen you, Yes, I will help you, I will uphold you with My righteous right hand" (Isaiah 41:10 NKJV).

"For I consider that the sufferings of this present time are not worthy to be compared with the glory which shall be revealed in us" (Romans 8:18 NKJV).

"And we know that all things work together for good to

those who love God, to those who are the called according to His purpose" (Romans 8:28 NKJV).

WHAT SITUATION IN YOUR LIFE LEFT BITTERNESS IN YOUR heart? Think about what you have learned from this adverse situation. God can use times like these to grow us spiritually. Allow Him to do that work in your life. How could your experience be used to help others?

MOTIVATION

Motivation is the general desire or willingness of someone to do something. For example, as leaders, we must "keep staff up to date and maintain interest and motivation." Synonyms for "motivation" are enthusiasm, drive, initiative, and determination. In order to help motivate others, we have to remain motivated ourselves.

Sometimes in certain areas of our lives we say, "My heart is just not in it." We may even feel we must fake it till we make it. Whatever you have to tell yourself in order to push through is what we strive to do. *Just Do It* as the Nike commercials say. We may need to be reminded—you've done this before, you've got this. You can do it! Thank God for dear ones who help remind us that this is not our first rodeo, and we can achieve what is set before us. We may just need to get in the rhythm.

It's the same in our faith. We need to remember all that God has previously done for us. He has never left or forsaken us, and He never will. Motivation is also defined as that which moves us toward action. As Christians, we should be motivated by His word to put our works into play. Right? "I desire to do Your will, O my God; Your law is within my heart" (Psalm 40:8). Later he wrote, "Whom have I in heaven but you? And earth has nothing I desire besides you" (Psalm 73:25).

The Bible actually has a good bit to say about motivation. The world is motivated by self. But as followers of Christ, we should be motivated by what pleases our Heavenly Father.

Our motivation as believers stems from a yearning to have peace with God (Romans 5:1; Philippians 4:7), to have His grace as well as hope (Romans 5:2; 1 John 5:13). The Christian views life through the lens of the future—being in the presence and glory of God (John 17:24), and this is our true motivation.

We are reminded in Colossians 3:23, "Whatever you do, work heartily, as for the Lord and not for men."

How do you remain motivated? Who are you helping to stay motivated? Give encouraging words to someone else today. You will surely be blessed.

NOTHING

The world today is a different place from the one I grew up in. I lived in Unity Community down a gravel road in West Carroll Parish, Louisiana. I remember our address was Rt. 1 Box 48C Pioneer, LA 71266. My grandmother, Lilla Oldham, lived right around the corner. My grandparents, Maureen and Cleophas Beebe, lived out in Green Community. I had a couple aunts who lived in our community and we all attended New Hope Church of God. We had close family friends like the Durbins, Ezells, Boykins, Honeycutts whom my folks played cards or dominoes with. The quartet practiced on Saturday nights while kids played music on the radio and just hung out. We were outside a lot—climbing trees and playing chase and catching lightning bugs in glass jars for fun. We saw all of our relatives often, even those who lived away would come in about once a year and sometimes more often. We would occasionally go visit them in Baton Rouge, Louisiana, Jackson, Mississippi, and even traveled up to Indiana.

I took this journey down memory lane AGAIN because of what we say too many times when we see our close friends and relatives at memorial services or visitations, "Let's not let the next time we talk or see one another be at an occasion like this." We always promise that it won't be... and yet it usually always repeats itself. Life is busy. We all feel like we meet ourselves coming too often.

When people ask me where I am from, I say Oak Grove, Louisiana. Now I have not lived in Oak Grove since 1991. So why am I still from there? Because it is home. Nothing separates us from our roots, where we were raised, and those people we have deep connections with, whether family or childhood friends.

It's like that with our spiritual life also. I was saved and baptized at a young age—eight, I believe. And yet over the years, I went astray, to say the least. Sad to say that I was not in church for over twenty-five years. But God brought me to a place in my life where I realized He was my only hope. Without Him, I am nothing.

Putting Him first and foremost in our lives means honoring Him as the top priority in our lives. Even in our darkest of times, He reminds us in Psalms 23:4 that, "Yea though I walk through the valley of the shadow of death, I fear no evil for thou art with me; Thy rod and thy staff they comfort me."

Nothing separates us from what we hold dear and sacred —our home, our family, our friends, our faith, hope and trust in Him.

> *So now I live with the confidence that there is nothing in the universe with the power to separate us from God's love. I'm convinced that his love will triumph over death, life's troubles, fallen angels, or dark rulers in the heavens. There is nothing in our present or future circumstances that can weaken his love.*

FAITH WILL FIND YOU

There is no power above us or beneath us—no power that could ever be found in the universe that can distance us from God's passionate love, which is lavished upon us through our Lord Jesus, the Anointed One (Romans 8:38-39 TPT).

Where do you find home today? What is your home base? The place where you find peace and comfort? Create space in your heart and life to have that safe place.

NOTICE

The word notice can be used as a verb or a noun. We have all most likely been put on notice before. There it is used as a noun meaning warning of something coming. It can also be used as a verb meaning "to become aware of" (e.g., have you noticed the change in the weather).

When we are saved, people notice a change in us. They see a change in our status and what we believe in and what we say and do. Notice it is not just what we say, but what we do. Our actions speak louder than words. They may see us attending church or serving in other capacities that are new to our lifestyle. There are some doubters out there. Some have called those of us who voice our faith in God through our regular posts, "Facebook preachers." They may call us out on our new lifestyle and doubt that we have really changed. They notice a change, but don't believe it is real. Only God knows if a real and thorough change has taken place.

Consider the following passages from Mark 14:68-70 TPT:

68 But Peter denied it, saying, "I don't have a clue what

you're talking about." Then he went out to the gateway of the courtyard and the rooster crowed.

69 When the servant girl noticed him, she said to all the bystanders, "I know this man is one of his followers!"

70 Once again, Peter denied it. A short time later, the bystanders said to him, "You must be one of them. You're a Galilean, like he is, for your accent proves it!"

The servant girl noticed that Peter was associated with Jesus, although Peter denied it. What do people notice about us—not just on social media but day by day as they work beside us? What do they notice when others push our buttons or treat us poorly or hurt us? Are we still a reflection of Christ? More importantly, what does Christ notice about how we are striving to be more like Him? Does He notice that we are chasing after Him or does He see us chasing after something else? Maybe something we have been chasing for a long time?

There comes a time in our lives when we must let go of the past and what our desires were before we were saved or totally dedicated to Christ. Then, and only then, do people NOTICE that we are a true reflection of Christ, not our flesh.

What do those around you notice about you? Your actions? Your words? Are you reflecting Christ in your everyday life? What about when someone offends you? How do you handle that?

OFFENDED

Our church series "Fully Known" got me to thinking… sometimes we think we know someone. We may "know of" them, but have not spent any time in conversation with them. We don't spend enough time with them to fully know them. I have had people snub me.

One day I saw a woman I knew from my past—we went to the same school many years ago. I knew some of her family. But I didn't know her at all and it became clearly evident. I said "Hey you are _____ , right? From _____ (somewhere I lived before). I know you. Remember me?" And I told her my name. She said, "Yes, I know who you are." Then she turned, got in her truck, and drove away. I stood there dumbfounded. That was the longest conversation I had ever had with her. What did I do to make her hate me? I also had someone who offended me this year. This person made some accusations about things very near and dear to me —family and my personal life. They said don't be offended, but I was.

Perceptions are a funny thing. And I don't mean, Ha Ha

funny. Others see in us what they believe in their minds, like it's dreamed up but not grounded in reality. I am still learning so much about life and, my Christian walk, but mostly about loving people—of all kinds. Even those who offend me.

In James 2 we are reminded, "My dear brothers and sisters, fellow believers in our glorious Lord Jesus Christ—how could we say that we have faith in Him and yet we favor one group of people above another? Suppose an influential man comes into your worship meeting wearing gold rings and expensive clothing, and also a homeless man in shabby clothes comes in. If you show special attention to the rich man in expensive clothes and say, "Here's a seat of honor for you right up front!" but you turn and say to the poor beggar dressed in rags, "You can stand over here," or "Sit over there on the floor in the back." Just as we are not to judge others by our perceptions, we should not be judged.

Everyone has trials. Everyone has something that they struggle with. If they are lucky, it's not more than one thing. We may sometimes judge by what we think others have that we don't. That may actually be envy. With assets come debt. With family comes responsibility. With successful relationships comes hard work and patience and accountability. Anything worth having is worth working for. These things don't happen because of magic. Favor comes from faithfulness. Prayer is a part of faithfulness. We must remain faithful even in the lean times. Even when we are hurt or offended.

Proverbs 18:19 says, "It is easier to conquer a strong city than to win back a friend whom you've offended. Their walls go up, making it nearly impossible to win them back." But James 5:16 tells us, "Confess and acknowledge how you have offended one another and then pray for one another to be instantly healed, for tremendous power is released through the passionate, heartfelt prayer of a godly believer!"

Just as I have been offended, I have offended, I'm sure. Lord, help me to only speak words that I don't need to take back. I have never claimed to be perfect—far from it. I am however, forgiven. God loves me and has done such a work in my life. I am forever grateful for His saving grace and His willingness to love me in spite of my human nature.

We never know what might be happening in someone else's life that might affect how they speak to others and even what they say. They may be "taking it out" on those around them without realizing it. It may be you doing that. Or it may be me.

Are you or allowing what's going on in your life drive how we speak to and treat others? How can you do a better job at showing grace to others by speaking kindly so we don't offend?

PASSION

Passion, a word that is underused, in my opinion. Although it has several meanings, we generally think of it when referring to how we feel about our significant other or how strongly we feel about something—being passionate about our work, hobby, or anything else we hold dear.

Passion is defined as a strong and barely controllable emotion. One example is "a man of impetuous passion." Impetuous means without thought or care. This could refer to a blind fit of anger. Other synonyms for passion include love, desire, or lust.

Another definition of passion is the suffering and death of Jesus. For example, "meditations on the Passion of Christ." Synonyms are crucifixion, agony, suffering. We don't hesitate to be passionate about our loved one or other causes we are driven to serve, but are we truly passionate about our Lord Jesus Christ? We may say we are, but how do we show it?

Psalm 63:4 says, "Daily I will worship you passionately and with all my heart. My arms will wave to you like banners of praise." If you followed me to work on weekdays, you might see my hands up some days as I praise and worship while preparing for my day. Pull beside me in the car and you might see me singing or drumming on my steering wheel as I drive. Personally, it has been very freeing to raise my hands to heaven when I am praising and worshiping the Lord. That is not limited to church services. Think about a baby when they are tired or wet or hungry or sick, they reach up to their mommy or daddy to pick them up. That's what I see as I lift my hands up to Him. Praying, Father lift me up. Save me from myself. Fill me with your spirit. More of you and less of me. I seek you Father this day. Walk and talk with me. Lead, guide, and direct my thoughts. Help others to see you in me and my actions.

Psalm 63:8 tells us that we are to have passion and cling to Christ. Because we feel His grip on our life, we should keep our soul close to His heart. One Sunday, Pastor Dallas talked about how chains can have us bound. He brought up that chains should not have us because that means we have no hope, but that we have the chains instead of them having us. That means that we can break free with God's help from that which binds us. He is our way maker and chain breaker. Let's be more passionate for Christ than we are for anything else. No one else has ever given more for you or me—His life on the cross for our sins.

How do you show that you are truly passionate about Christ? Do others want to be His follower because of what they see in you?

PATIENCE

Patience is the capacity to accept or tolerate delay, trouble, or suffering without getting angry or upset. It is one of my many weaknesses. Waiting . . . on His timing. Guns N' Roses even has a song, "Patience." Give it a listen. It's kind of sweet. I digress . . . back to patience.

Patience is a virtue and talked about throughout the Bible in the Old and New Testaments. According to 1 Samuel, "Lack of patience can cause you to miss blessings." I can share from personal experience that when you try to make things happen on your timeline, it will not work out as you planned. In Genesis 29:20 NIV it says, "So Jacob served seven years for Rachel, and they seemed to him but a few days because of the love he had for her." That is some patience there. Not only that, but he was tricked and got the older sister, Leah, first. Then he had to serve again for another seven years to have Rachel.

The story of Abraham and Sarah required patience as they waited on the promise of a child that was not fulfilled until she was ninety-nine years old. They waited twenty-five years for the birth of Isaac.

Romans 8:25-28 NIV says:

But if we hope for what we do not yet have, we wait for it patiently. In the same way, the Spirit helps us in our weakness. We do not know what we ought to pray for, but the Spirit himself intercedes for us through wordless groans. And he who searches our hearts knows the mind of the Spirit, because the Spirit intercedes for God's people in accordance with the will of God. And we know that in all things God works for the good of those who love him, who have been called according to his purpose.

You see, we may have ideas about what we think is best for our life, but if we are living outside of the perfect will of God, we may crash and burn, so to speak. We must WAIT on Him and His timing for our life.

We all live busy lives. It seems that we are always in a hurry. We pick up supper at the drive-thru window. We get cash from the ATM and apply for credit online. In addition to things like instant potatoes, we can even call in and pick up our groceries curbside. As we age, we may have to slow down a bit and even rest more often to keep on trucking. We find it difficult to slow down, unless we have to because we have not become convinced that allowing things to unfold in their own time is best.

Many times, the lesson and/or blessing is in the waiting. God will redirect our path if we look to Him for our guidance. Stay in tune with God. Daily ask, "God, what are you saying? What are you doing? What would you have me do?" Don't look at what others do or say or have. God's plan for each of us is personalized. It is differentiated. Don't miss the blessings He has for you because of your impatience to have what you want when you want it. Pray constantly. Believe always. Have faith that His plan is best for your life.

"Again I say unto you, That if two of you shall agree on earth as touching anything that they shall ask, it shall be done for them of my Father which is in heaven" (Matthew 18:19 KJV).

WHAT ARE YOU BELIEVING FOR IN PRAYER? HAVE YOU ASKED friends to agree with you over that specifically? If not, do so believing it will be done. But remember, it will be in God's time, so be patient.

Prayer group at LifeChurch.LA in Ruston, LA

PREPARATION

God uses everything in our life to prepare us for something good in our present or future. Every tear that falls, every experience that we go through, God hears and sees. He hurts when we hurt.

Have you ever had those people in your life for whom you just hurt? I mean, we all do. When our children hurt, we hurt with them. Our hearts break. We even have those feelings for close friends—when they suffer our hearts do, too. We have a heaviness on our heart for them—their health, spiritual walk, finances, family. We pray for them and check on them. I am blessed to have friends like that in my life.

"So, my beloved friends, with all that you have to look forward to, may you be eager to be found living pure lives *when you come into his presence*, without blemish and filled with peace" (2 Peter 3:14).

All throughout the Bible there were preparations made—before Jesus' birth, before Passover, before the Last Supper, prior to His crucifixion and His resurrection. For each of these times in the Bible, there were unknown blessings that would result from the upcoming events.

FAITH WILL FIND YOU

As horrific as Jesus' crucifixion was, we are all blessed to have His blood, His brokenness, and ultimately His death that covers our sins, our transgressions, our failures. Creation was preparation for our world today. It has transitioned over time. It doesn't take much to appreciate the beauty of our earth if we will slow down long enough to enjoy it.

As I recently enjoyed a trip to the Montana mountains, I relished the gorgeous skies, snow-capped mountains, and wildlife. It is like layer upon layer of beauty revealed a little at a time. It did my heart, mind, and soul good to get away, to experience solitude with nature hidden away high above worries or cares of what I left behind. The air was crisp and clear, and it honestly felt like God was near. He is near when we slow down enough to realize it.

God continues to grow my patience. He is telling me loud and clear to slow down and trust Him in EVERY part of my life. He has my back. He has yours. The preparation for us is reading His word and praying. That is how we are more prepared for anything that may cross our path or give us reason to stress or doubt or fear. We need to remember that we are too blessed to be stressed. I like the saying that stressing means we are not trusting God.

We need to constantly remind ourselves what Proverbs 16 says: "Go ahead and make all the plans you want, but it's the Lord who will ultimately direct your steps. We are all in love with our own opinions, convinced they're correct. But the Lord is in the midst of us, testing and probing our every motive. Before you do anything, put your trust totally in God and not in yourself. Then every plan you make will succeed."

JEANANNE OLDHAM

Are you trusting God for your future? Are you allowing Him to direct your steps? Do you hear Him? Do you listen and heed his commandment?

PRESENCE

"You're my place of quiet retreat, and your wrap-around presence becomes my shield as I wrap myself in your word" (Psalm 119:114).

This verse is one of my favorites because of the visual it creates in my mind when I read it and the comfort it gives me. There are many things people claim give them comfort—food, bed, a soft quilt, a shoulder to cry on, or a hand to hold. Being held brings comfort from a friend or loved one. It is comforting to be in the company of others whom we care about. However, quickly we turn to worldly things to retreat and shield ourselves from hurtful words, stress or anxiety, or whatever we are dealing with; and it does not make the world go away.

Remember, the old song sung by both Eddy Arnold and Elvis Presley, "Make the World Go Away?" You can close your eyes and try any of these earthly comforts, but when you open your eyes—yep, it's still there. The world and those things that don't bring us peace.

There is only one way to have peace over the stresses of this life and that is the everlasting wrap-around presence of

God. He is the peace that passes ALL understanding. If His presence, the Holy Spirit, is wrapped around you, it goes with you. It schools us and guides us in how we respond to others. We arm ourselves with His word. We speak it from our mouth.

Even Henry Ford recognized the key when he said, "Those who walk with God always reach their destination."

In John 8:12, Jesus spoke to the people once more and said, "I am the light of the world. If you follow me, you won't have to walk in darkness, because you will have the light that leads to life."

Micah 6:8 ISV reminds me that "He has made it clear to me, mortal man, what is good and what the LORD is requiring from me— is to act with justice, to treasure the LORD's gracious love, and to walk humbly in the company of your God."

How can you allow God's wrap-around presence in your life more? What do you think will happen when you begin to sit quietly in His presence? Give it a try. Speak His word and hold fast to those truths for your life.

RAW

I wonder if we were all very honest, how many of us would admit that we have had this thought: If I died today, would it matter to anyone? Who would miss us? Who would wish they had told us how they really felt about us? Is there anyone who would have regrets about not telling us their true feelings? Would there be those who wished they would have reached out to us when they saw we were hurting, but didn't?

Those are not godly thoughts, but they are raw and they are real. Many of us have had them at some time in our lives. The devil is alive and well, folks. His goal is to kill or defeat us or, if he can, have us weigh in on our own self-destruction. It is his goal in life.

I know I have always felt I could talk to our Heavenly Father any time, but then at times I thought I could shield some of my innermost thoughts from him. How ridiculous is that? He knows our every thought, our hopes, and dreams. He knows our fears, our concerns, our worries, and the doubt that plagues us even when we silence them.

The enemy tries to make us feel that we don't matter in

this world. Maybe that special someone you believed is the one is showing some signs of change or distance. Maybe friends are too busy to notice your need. Satan tries to tell us we are not worthy of love or joy or happiness. He tries to tell us we don't matter to anyone, even when we know that is not true. Know this. . . he is wrong. He is a liar. *That* is something you can believe!

Jeremiah 29:11 AMP tells us, "'For I know the plans *and* thoughts that I have for you,' says the Lord, 'plans for peace *and* well-being and not for disaster, to give you a future and a hope.'" We always have hope in Him, no matter what is going on in our life. I am also reminded in Ephesians 2:10 ESV that, "we are his workmanship, created in Christ Jesus for good works, which God prepared beforehand, that we should walk in them."

Walk it out. Talk it out with the Father. Remember the "Footprints in the Sand" poem. We look at our life and think He has forsaken us, but that one set of footprints is when He carried us. No matter who has walked out on you. No matter who has disrespected you or talked about you behind your back. No matter the drama or hatred that surrounds you . . .

find your peace in Him. Be raw and real with Him so you can be found.

Have you spoken with God about His plans for your life? Do you know your purpose? If not, talk with him today. He is waiting.

FAITH WILL FIND YOU

Mountain Time Bozeman, Montana October 2018

REBUKE

Most of us have heard of "stinkin' thinkin.'" No, it's not in the Webster's dictionary, but it is a real term. Especially for those of us who have those voices in our heads that attempt to tell us we are not worthy, not able, not skilled, not valued, not godly, not honest, not truthful, and certainly not forgiven. The voice tells us we are inadequate or not enough. Remember, John 10:10? You know what he does—comes to kill, steal, and destroy. We are also warned in Romans 16:17 to watch out for those who cause divisions. In John 8:44 NIV reminds us "You belong to your father, the devil, and you want to carry out your father's desires. He was a murderer from the beginning, not holding to the truth, for there is no truth in him. When he lies, he speaks his native language, for he is a liar and the father of lies."

When these accusations or thoughts come at us, there is only one response—REBUKE the devil! Speak truths over your life, your family, your relationships, your mind, your thoughts. Speak aloud. I am forgiven of all my sins and washed by the Blood. I am a new creature in Christ. I am blessed and redeemed from the curse of the law. I am the head and not the tail . . . above and not beneath. I am strong in the Lord. I am dead to sin. I am joint heirs with Christ. Plead the blood of Jesus—the devil hates it when we plead the blood—over every aspect of your life. Pray this while believing Romans 16:20 NIV, "The God of peace will soon crush Satan under your feet. The grace of our Lord Jesus be with you." You are enough.

When Jesus rebuked someone or something, he demanded, in effect, on God's authority, that it cease and desist. Winds quieted. Demons exorcised. Fevers dismissed.

Remember this when you are actively seeking out the Lord and His plan for your life—Satan will try to come against you. He will use others to make accusations and place doubt in your mind. This is why an intimate relationship with God is so very important. Lisa Bevere says, "Our identity is like so much treasure hidden deep within him. We discover who we are in the revelation of whose we are." Keep marching on and remember, we are who He says we are.

WHAT DO YOU NEED TO REBUKE FROM YOUR LIFE? SPEAK aloud to that. Quote God's word over your family, your children, your job, your finances—every aspect of your life.

REDEMPTION

An act of redeeming or atoning for a fault or mistake or deliverance; rescue.

There are several movies about redemption—several songs, even a band. What does it mean to be redeemed? One may think about freedom from bondage—from a relationship, marriage, job, or family that held you back or kept you from being who you wanted to be. Maybe even an addiction or bad habit prevented you from living out your purpose.

Freedom comes from being delivered from those chains that bind you. Ironically, once freed, we wonder why we waited so long to take that step into freedom. It may have been fear or doubt that we could make the change, or maybe just fear of the unknown.

"Since a great price was paid for your redemption, stop having the mind-set of a slave" (1 Corinthians 7:23). As Christians we know about the miraculous redemption that saved us from a lifetime of sin. The brokenness of Jesus' body and the blood he shed for us brought redemption in our life. He paid the ultimate price for us. There are many stories in the Bible about those who were redeemed. There's Ruth, whose redemption brought her into the lineage of King David and the Lord Jesus Christ. One of my favorites is the story Jesus told about the man who left the ninety-nine to find the one lost sheep. A feast was then prepared to celebrate the redemption of the sheep that was found.

You know the story of the prodigal son and how the celebration unfolded for the one that returned. The opportunity to be redeemed is available to everyone. If or when we accept His love, His grace, His mercy, and His saving grace, we become redeemed. It is there for the asking. Don't allow anything to stand between you and His love.

"Since we are now joined to Christ, we have been given the treasures of redemption by his blood—the total cancellation of our sins—all because of the cascading riches of his grace"

(Ephesians 1:7).

Do you doubt how much God loves you? Don't! You are the one he would leave the fold for. Seek Him today.

REFLECT, RECALL, REMEMBER

On the last day of the year, I like to reflect on where I have been spiritually, emotionally, and physically over the last twelve months. I think about the paths that I took, unfortunately not always the road less traveled. However, God and His infinite wisdom continue to guide and protect me. Although His guidance has been the source of some disappointment and hurt over the last couple years, I know it is all a part of God's customized plan for me. His plans are always better for us than anything we can imagine. As the old saying goes, "No pain, no gain." The hurt and disappointments are not his fault, they are mine and, honestly, not always mine alone. I cannot guide my own ship without Christ as my Captain. In spite of knowing that, I sometimes forge ahead into the stormy waters and then wonder why I cry over what's happened in my life.

It is important for us to recall all the things that God has done in our lives—our *whole* lives. Our focus should be on what favor He has provided and not the few things that we feel may be missing. Maybe those few things are not in His plan for us. Maybe He has not brought those things across our

FAITH WILL FIND YOU

path for a reason. Maybe we are not ready. It is all about trusting in God's timing.

This is what the Lord says: He who made a way through the sea, a path through the mighty waters, "Forget the former things; do not dwell on the past. See, I am doing a new thing! Now it springs up; do you not perceive it? I am making a way in the wilderness and streams in the wasteland" (Isaiah 43:16, 18-19 NIV).

As I remembered God's faithfulness I give thanks. I have all the essentials to live a happy life and MORE! I have a roof over my head, food to eat, family, friends, and a job I love dearly. My health is good (although I could stand to lose a few pounds). I have a wonderful church family and, most importantly, I have a God who cares for me. He saved me from myself.

Thank you, Jesus, for your mercy and grace! You allowed me back into the fold. Honestly, the rains in my life brought me back, mainly losing my sweet Daddy—my rock.

I want to encourage those who are depressed, weighed down with grief or loss or sadness of any kind, don't hesitate to find a Christian counselor or pastor to help you walk through this dark time. It saved my life—literally—and actually got me back into church in a way I had never experienced before.

In Deuteronomy 31:8 we are reminded, "Do not be afraid or discouraged, for the LORD will personally go ahead of you. He will be with you; he will neither fail you nor abandon you."

Let's leave the past where it is, behind us. Let us move forward in the confidence that He goes before us clearing the path. In the devotional book, *My Utmost for His Highest* by Oswald Chambers, given to me by my sweet friend, Shelby Blackstock, it says that "God will garrison where we have failed to. He will watch lest things trip us up again into failure, as they assuredly would do if He were not our rereward. Let the past sleep, but let it sleep on the bosom of Christ." Garrison means fortified strong—Christ is always that for us, even at our weakest. Rereward is rear coverage, so to speak. So as we move into a new year, let us remember He goes before us and He has our back.

"You've gone into my future to prepare the way, and in kindness you follow behind me to spare me from the harm of my past. With your hand of love upon my life, you impart a blessing to me" (Psalm 139:5).

TAKE SOME TIME IN THE STILLNESS OF GOD'S LOVE TO reflect about your past. What needs to be left behind? Where can you make small changes that will have a large impact on your future? It is time to move forward with Christ, leading and guiding.

FAITH WILL FIND YOU

Sparkman, Arkansas Credit: Seth Easterling

REJECTION

Unfortunately, we have all experienced a cold shoulder, and I am not talking about the weather. I am speaking about being caught off guard by someone you trusted and felt that they had your best interest at heart—until you learned they didn't.

We think we know people. We believe what they say to us. However, we may interpret what they say to mean something different because it is what WE want to believe.

Deception also comes into play. Are those within our circle of trust honest about their affections or intentions? Rejection hurts whether it is intended or not. The lack of open communication can be the culprit of mixed messages that leads to rejection. It stings. No matter how many times you have survived the hurt, no matter your age—it takes a while to heal. It may cause you to build walls around your heart. It may leave you with baggage that you cannot unload.

Rejection "communicates the sense to somebody that they're not loved or not wanted, or not in some way valued." This definition was coined by Geraldine Downey, Ph.D., a professor at Columbia University. Rejection comes from missing that promotion or new job you applied for. It can be social rejection by your peers or a group of people you want to be connected with, but they shun you. It can be asking someone out and hearing, "No, thank you." The majority of the damage from rejection comes from what happens once you begin to expect rejection and begin that negative self-talk. Those comments are planted in our heads from the one and only Satan.

There's even a Rejection Hotline—wish I had known that! However, the best way to overcome rejection is to make sure you are staying in the presence of God and keeping your dreams and thoughts aligned with His complete will. We are sometimes selfish and want what we want when we want it. It has been pointed out to me—and I agree—that I am impatient. I think we all are to a certain extent. Especially when we forget to trust our creator—you know, the man with the plan.

It could be that the rejection from others is an answer from God. Does it hurt? Well, certainly it does. I trust until someone proves that they are not trustworthy. We must be careful about who we allow in our circle of trust. What is their purpose for being in our life? That is something to pray fervently over, for sure.

Jesus was rejected, despised, and persecuted here on earth.

Remember this: "The stone that the builders rejected has become the cornerstone" (Psalm 118:22 ESV).

"Come and hear, all you who fear God, and I will tell what he has done for my soul. I cried to him with my mouth, and high praise was on my tongue. If I had cherished iniquity in my heart, the Lord would not have listened. But truly God has listened; he has attended to the voice of my prayer. Blessed be God, because he has not rejected my prayer or removed his steadfast love from me" (Psalms 66:16-20 BSB).

Remember that rejection can be God's way of protecting you. Thank him today for his protection over your life. Allow him to heal your hurting heart. Won't you have a heart-talk with Him today? He is our ultimate healer.

RELATIONSHIP

What is a relationship? It is the way in which two or more people or organizations regard and behave toward each other. There are many different types of relationships: tenant-landlord, mother-son, father-daughter, husband-wife, employee-employer, boyfriend-girlfriend, friend-friend, and on and on.

Something funny happened while researching what relationship means on Google . . . You may have heard the term "friends with benefits" (FWB). Granted it's not scriptural nor does it align with God's teachings in any way, but I have a point to make—stay with me. A FWB does not always pertain to physical comfort but emotional as well. It basically means there is no commitment and anything goes. Me, I am not a fan of this but I do understand it. There is too much of the unknown and feelings that may be hurt along the way.

Perceptions of what a relationship is or isn't, including whether the relationship exists at all, differ from person to person. This is determined by the expectations each party has about what they are looking for in the relationship. The standards on which the relationship is "built" is most important for success. Additionally, you need to consider the same values of how that union is built and what values/moral it is built on. Do you get where I am going with this?

According to my Google search, there are five stages of a relationship. First is Attraction. Next, Reality sets in. Then, Disappointment, Stability, and finally, Commitment.

Although friendship and other relationship success is important in our lives, the one most important is our relationship with Jesus Christ. What are our expectations of that one? Is it based on the Word? Or on the hope that we can escape pain and suffering at all costs? As I noted above about other relationships, it is important that EACH party have the same expectations and values about the merger. What does God expect of us? Are we fulfilling that? What are the benefits of having that intimate relationship with God? There are many!

Lisa Bevere says, "Loving God should always translate into loving others well." Serving God is one of the greatest things we have been given by the Lord to do. So, our attitude about serving God should be one that is reflective of Psalm 100:2 (NKJV): "Serve the Lord with gladness; Come before His presence with singing." This will bring ultimate joy to our lives. Matthew 22:37-40 reminds us that Jesus said, "'Love the Lord your God with every passion of your heart, with all the energy of your being, and with every thought that is within you. This is the great and supreme commandment. And the second is like it in importance: 'You must love your friend in the same way you love yourself.' Contained within these commandments to love you will find all the meaning of the Law and the Prophets."Yes, even when we are hurting, push through and do what God expects us to do. We may feel like we are faking it a bit, but the reward will come through."

The most important relationship status for each of us is a strong, well-founded, minute-by-minute merger with God, our Maker, our Savior, our Redeemer. I love the song by Natalie Grant, "More than Anything." The chorus says this:

Help me want the healer more than the healing
Help me want the savior more than the saving
Help me want the giver more than the giving
Oh help me want you Jesus more than anything

James 4:6-10 ESV tells us that He gives us more grace. "God opposes the proud, but gives grace to the humble. Submit yourselves therefore to God. Resist the devil, and he will flee from you. Draw near to God, and He will draw near to you. Cleanse your hands, you sinners, and purify your hearts, you double-minded. Be wretched and mourn and weep. Let your laughter be turned to mourning and your joy to gloom. Humble yourselves before the Lord, and He will exalt you."

As new Christians, we had that initial attraction, the Holy Spirit, that drew us in. Then reality set in and we may have experienced disappointment—a death, a breakup, rejection, a setback of some sort may have caused us to doubt our relationship with God. Then, when we came through the other side, stronger and all the better for the victory in the struggle; we understood the stability and gains from walking with Him.

Then and only then could we have the commitment to Him. The pain, the hurts, the struggles—they grow us, and yes, sometimes stretch us WAY beyond where we ever thought we would or could be. The way we give back is to support and pray for others as they walk down a similar rocky path of suffering. Then, and only then, can we know what it's like to trust in Jesus. If we never go through anything, how do we know? Remember, God already knows all about us. He wants us to know Him.

The Bible says God is at work in everyone's life: "So that they should seek the Lord, in the hope that they might grope for Him and find Him, though He is not far from each one of us" (Acts 17:27 NASB). The best relationship is that of a genuine friendship based on honesty and truth. Our Heavenly Father is always our best option as a true friend, he is not just a friend with benefits as a convenience. The benefits of a relationship with Him far outweighs — anything.

ARE YOU HOLDING ONTO FRIENDSHIPS THAT HAVE NO benefits? Are you the kind of friend that you hope to have? The benefit of friendship is that we have a companion who truly cares for us.

One that we take for granted too often is Jesus our forever friend. Won't you check out His benefits?

R-E-S-P-E-C-T

These thoughts came after the passing of the DIVA of soul—Aretha Franklin. Respect today is not honored as much as it was in the past. People's right to speak has overshadowed the respect that many of us were taught in our generation. Too many people believe their right of speech trumps what their words do to others. Respect, like love, is not a feeling; it is a choice. Romans 12:10 tells us to "love one another with brotherly affection. Outdo one another in showing honor."

Respect can mean different things to different people. What does it mean to you? The golden rule, do unto others as you would have them do unto you (Matthew 7:12), is one we quote a lot. I hear my children correct their children (my grands) any time they do not say, "Yes/No ma'am" or "Yes/No sir" to adults. That is certainly a form of respect and comes from Ephesians 6:1-3 when it says to honor your father and mother and obey them.

As adults, we earn respect by giving it to others. You must give it in order to receive it. In the workplace, we respect people for the service or job they do, knowing full well we are not willing to make the sacrifices or shoulder the responsibilities they have to face daily. Respect is an overall evaluation you give others based on how you feel they are living their life. Some are quick to evaluate or judge others, but may not look in the mirror and evaluate themselves (self-respect). It is easier sometimes to look at others instead of looking within.

Most of us show respect in many ways—we pull over on the side of the road when we meet a funeral procession. We open doors for others. We take other's feelings into consideration. We listen. Philippians 2:3 HCSB reminds us to "do nothing from rivalry or conceit, but in humility count others more significant than yourselves." Be nice. Be kind. Be what others refuse to be to you. Take the high road or the road less traveled.

Most importantly, how do we respect our Savior? One of the ten commandments is not to use the Lord's name in vain. There has been much debate about what that really means. When we think of Jesus, another word for respect is honor. How do we honor Him? Psalm 86:9-11 says, "All nations whom You have made shall come and worship before You, O Lord, and they shall glorify Your name. For You are great and do wondrous deeds; You alone are God. Teach me Your way, O LORD; I will walk in Your truth; Unite my heart to fear Your name."

1 Corinthians 10:31 tells us to do all things to the glory of God. Proverbs 3:9 reminds us to honor God with our wealth, giving the first fruits of our produce. In other words, tithe. The first ten percent is His already—that's how I see it. Matthew 22:37 ESV commands us, "You shall love the Lord your God with all your heart and with all your soul and with all your mind." Love-honor-respect our Father.

FAITH WILL FIND YOU

How are you respecting God the Father? How will you show Him more love? Find more ways to honor him. He loves you so much!

RESTRUNG

Guitars, violins, fiddles, and other string instruments need to be restrung from time to time. But what happens to the old strings—can they be repurposed? Yesterday, I saw how they can be. Although they served their purpose for that instrument, I saw a young woman who took those old strings and made jewelry—very beautiful pieces: necklaces, earrings, and bracelets. It brought to my mind how God will take our broken strings—out of tune with right, living in the wrong—and restring us. He changes out the old for the new. In being restrung, He gives us a new tune, one that is aligned with His Word, His promises, His plan for our life. When we are saved or come back into fellowship with Christ, old things have passed away. 2 Corinthians 5:17 NKJV tells us, "Therefore, if anyone *is* in Christ, *he is* a new creation; old things have passed away; behold, all things have become new [italics added]."

Have a blessed day. Praise His Holy Name on a daily basis! Offer thanksgiving for all He has done in your life! Don't forget to be blessed by blessing someone else.

FAITH WILL FIND YOU

People should be able to see a different us. Shouldn't they? If we have been restrung in Christ, we are His and He is ours. Our light and our life should reflect that. What are others seeing in you today? How can you allow a work that seemingly "restrings" who you are?

Restrung Image by Nancy Bell

SAFE AND SECURE

When we hear storm or tornado sirens go off, it shakes our sense of safety. When the wind whips and limbs and trees begin to fall, we do not feel secure. I remember one night in particular . . ..

The sirens began around 2:00 a.m. First came the Code Red Alert calls about thunderstorms in our area. Then the tornado sirens and more calls and alerts about the dangerous storm. "Take cover!" was the recommendation. Honestly, we were hearing so many sirens with all the rainstorms that I remained in bed. I said, "Lord, I am in my safe place with you." Thankfully, I awoke the next morning to no damage, not even any downed trees, just no power. However, other parts of my town, Ruston, Louisiana, were not so fortunate. We had extensive damage north of me near I-20 and two fatalities. Many prayers for Ruston, Louisiana went out that day (4/24/19) with heavy hearts for all of those affected and comfort and peace for the lives lost.

I love to read Psalm 91. The whole chapter is great, but in reference to feeling safe and secure in Christ, note the following verses that assure us we are safe and secure in Christ.

> *He's the hope that holds me and the Stronghold to shelter me, the only God for me, and my great confidence. His massive arms are wrapped around you, protecting you. You can run under his covering of majesty and hide. His arms of faithfulness are a shield keeping you from harm. Even in a time of disaster, with thousands and thousands being killed, you will remain unscathed and unharmed. God sends angels with special orders to protect you wherever you go, defending you from all harm. You'll even walk unharmed among the fiercest powers of darkness, trampling every one of them beneath your feet!*
> *For here is what the Lord has spoken to me: "Because you have delighted in me as my great lover, I will greatly protect you. I will set you in a high place, safe and secure before my face.*
> *I will answer your cry for help every time you pray, and you will find and feel my presence even in your time of pressure and trouble. I will be your glorious hero and give you a feast."*

WHERE DO YOU FIND PROTECTION? DO YOU TRUST GOD TO keep you safe? Rest in the assurances in His word today.

SCARS

Three years ago, I was moving a ceramic flower pot on the back porch when I suddenly dropped it. It broke instantly, and then I tripped and fell on it, cutting my right thigh wide open. I was home alone so I wrapped my injury in a towel and drove myself to the ER where I received 14 stitches. I was only into my second year of my principalship so I did not stay off my leg and infection set in. My doctor threatened to admit me to the hospital if the infection spread any further. It left quite an ugly scar; I am actually quite self-conscious of it now and try to keep it covered.

One day, I was wearing shorts, and as I looked down at my scar, I realized there's not really any covering it up so I should not worry about covering it—I learned a valuable lesson from that scary event and the mark that it left. It is part of who I am.

WE TRY TO COVER UP THE SCARS ON OUR HEARTS AND MINDS.

We hide our imperfections as a protective barrier so that others do not see how we hurt or what we struggle with. We are a proud people and we try to portray to others that we are fine and life is good. Sometimes we may learn that generations of our family faced demons of anxiety and stress to the extreme. Years of hidden emotional issues were buried in pride and shame. Most of us have events we experience that give us emotional scars. Mainly because we do not process them. We do not get closure. Sometimes we never tell the person who caused our pain how we are feeling, so we carry it. It rears its ugly head in various ways—high blood pressure, anxiety, sadness, depression, low or high heart rate, adrenaline level, and the list does not stop here.

But His word gives us hope in all situations. Psalm 147:3 NIV tells us, "He heals the brokenhearted and binds up their wounds." And then John 14:27 says, "Peace I leave with you; my peace I give to you. Not as the world gives do I give to you. Let know your hearts be troubled, neither let them be afraid."

Jenn Johnson of Bethel Church has a great message about Emotional Healing. The high points of the message are:

First, know your triggers. She addresses anger in this message. She says it covers a multitude of emotions—hurt, fear, and sadness.

Next, figure out what happened and why. Then, give the other person an opportunity to clear up what happened. If they don't know how it's affecting you, then it cannot be resolved.

Finally, and this is important, when you have done all you can within your power, stand on God's promises and let it go!

Forgiveness is a process with the Holy Spirit. The healing comes over time. Pray to receive a sound mind and a peace over the hurt that is still affecting you. If you have received the gift of praying in tongues, do that. Jenn refers to our love language as our secret Ninja weapon. Pray for alignment of your mind and life with His. You may need to do this. Close your eyes and picture God's hands, place that sadness in His hands and let it go.

The Holy Spirit will facilitate healing for you. Let go of the pain. Don't let them (the person or persons who hurt you) owe you anything. The Holy Spirit tells us to stay in the game. We have to allow Him to help us walk it out. Let God have it. Ask the Holy Spirit to tell you what lies you are believing, but then ask for the truth about who are you in Him to be revealed. Believe the truth that the Holy Spirit reveals to you, not the lies of the enemy.

YOU AND JESUS HAVE THIS! OUR SCARS MAKE US WHO WE are.

Aren't you thankful for His scars that gave us the forgiveness that we did not deserve?

Are you carrying anything today that you need to let go of? Find the root of the problem. Address it, and then let it go. Be thankful for your scars today. Share your story. You never know how many others will be blessed.

SCATTERED

Life is so busy . . . and complicated. And yes, sometimes confusing. Our brains are multi-tasking, trying to process all that we need to be doing at work or personally, dwelling on thoughts and even future plans we may be dreaming of.

Sometimes we may feel like we would lose our head if it were not attached to our body. We are forgetful and lose things, we become disorganized—this does not only happen to those who are aging, but also to those who are overwhelmed. It may cause us to feel as if we are losing our way, like we are a lost cause or, yes, that we are cracking up. Life is hard! There are lots of choices in life, leaving us as scattered as the fall leaves.

We speak of scattered showers. As parents we remember the scattered toys—maybe blocks, cars, trucks, Legos or dolls—and the clothes tossed throughout the house when our children were small. Scattered is also used to describe someone who is reckless or careless in his/her actions or coming off the effects of drug consumption. Scattered also means quickly moving apart upon someone's arrival, like when the police arrive. Some may even refer to us as scatterbrained.

The word scattered is found sixty-nine times in the King James Version of the Bible. It mentions scattered sheep, scattered seeds, and the scattering of people. In Mark 14 Jesus said to them, "All of you will be made to stumble because of Me this night, for it is written: 'I will strike the Shepherd, And the sheep will be scattered.'"

This was when Peter and other disciples were declaring their allegiance to Jesus. They denied that they would ever be unloyal or scattered from Him. Jesus told Peter, "Before the rooster crows, you will deny me three times." Well, we all know what happened. Jesus was correct and Peter denied knowing Jesus not once, not twice, but three times.

In Ezekiel 34, God's Message came to me:

Son of man, prophesy against the shepherd-leaders of Israel. Yes, prophesy! Tell those shepherds, 'God, the Master, says: Doom to you shepherds of Israel, feeding your own mouths! Aren't shepherds supposed to feed sheep? You drink the milk, you make clothes from the wool, you roast the lambs, but you don't feed the sheep. You don't build up the weak ones, don't heal the sick, don't doctor the injured, don't go after the strays, don't look for the lost. You bully and badger them. And now they're scattered every which way because there was no shepherd—scattered and easy pickings for wolves and coyotes. Scattered—*my sheep!*—exposed and vulnerable across mountains and hills. My sheep scattered all over the world, and no one out looking for them!

There are times when we need to re-evaluate our lives and make changes. If we are too scattered in our lives, we may be everywhere and nowhere all at the same time. We may need to take a step back and determine our priorities, making a new plan in consideration of what is really important in our lives—not letting life run us, but rather letting God lead and guide us.

We may have operated a certain way all our lives, but one day, if we don't slow down and put first thing's first, we may live to regret our choices. Even worse, we may not live to be able to have those regrets. He is our Shepherd and we are His sheep. Shouldn't our lives reflect that? Is it evident in our day-to-day actions?

Let's not allow ourselves to be the enemy's easy pickings because that's what happens when our priorities are screwed up. The devil loves it when we are scattered from our Father and we are disorganized in our life. If we don't have a clear direction, he will try to steer us. It won't be pretty, and it won't end as the good Lord intended, for sure.

I often feel scattered when so many things come at me at once. People are never as together as they seem—that surely includes me. Never forget that! There is a big old world out there similar to a ship. What is the ship guided by? A rudder—small but effective.

In James 3:4 it says, "Look at the ships also: though they are driven by strong winds, they are guided by a very small rudder whenever the will of the pilot directs." I ask you today, who is directing your ship?

WHAT IS EVIDENT IN OUR LIVES FROM OTHERS? DO THEY SEE us as a sheep following our Shepherd? Who or what is steering our life?

SEASONS

The Bible tells us in Ecclesiastes 3:1, "For everything there is a season." It also tells us in verse 11, "[God] has made everything beautiful in its time."

Speaking about timing—waiting on someone else's growth is the patience I speak often about. I love how the Holy Spirit orchestrates work in our lives. I began writing a couple days ago about protection. I was struggling with the coming together about something prophesied over my life. I didn't know how to get the point across in the right way.

As most have experienced, I too have had a season of darkness. Last year, change came in a big way. One in which I had to put my trust in the One and Only in actions instead of words alone. It has been much like a rollercoaster since then. I feel that I am on the "struggle bus" (love this term my Pastor, Dallas Witt, uses) and can't get off. Pastor preached today about how seasons of darkness in our lives give us so many feelings. During that season, we are not feeling very thankful. In fact, most likely just the opposite.

There are characters all through the Bible who experienced misery and disappointment. There's Job who pleaded to God when he lost his prosperity. He questioned God, but still remained faithful. Do we only love God because He blesses us? Job continued to love God in the midst of his trials, although he questioned God's purpose and reasoning.

Psalm 37:7 says, "Be still in the presence of the Lord, and wait patiently for him to act."

Wait patiently in the meantime. During this season of waiting, trust God. He may be pruning or removing what is not needed for your next season. He is making you ready so let Him work on His timeline.

There are also accounts of people such as Joseph, Abraham, and Hannah who demonstrated their faithfulness during adversity. Their seasons, like ours, came into a new time. God uses each and every season to grow us into who He has intended us to become. You see, our waiting is ongoing. He wants us to be able to wait, well, maybe for the rest of our lives. This is a scary thought for those of us who struggle with patience.

God's plan for us is His best plan for us. I generally have a Plan A, B, C, and D. God's plan for us is always Plan A—a plan of excellence and goodness filled with mercy and grace through our waiting and our struggles. He will bless us in our season of waiting. He will bless us in our season of darkness. He will bless us in our season of faithfulness. Keep the faith. Psalm 5:3 reminds us that "Each morning I bring my request to you and wait expectantly." God is forever listening and knows exactly where we are spiritually, emotionally, and physically. He has NEVER forgotten you. Never doubt that.

We all live in a season of busyness. It is a product of our culture. However, it is not something that we should chase after. We should always be chasing after our Savior. The key to success in every season is seeking God from every direction, from the time your feet hit the floor each morning until you fall into bed each evening.

This is from a dear friend, Pat Hutson Bruner. I have edited it to apply to each of you:

"God has a new trajectory for your life. His love for you is keeping you in a cocoon unto Him until the reveal of your future is ready. That's His way of protecting us. In the meantime, His grace covers you and me."

WHATEVER SEASON YOU ARE LIVING IN? TAKE HEART IN HIS Word. Proverbs 4:6 NIV tells us, "Do not forsake wisdom, and she will protect you; love her, and she will watch over you."

Jonesboro-Hodge Elementary courtyard in bloom

SOLITUDE

My daughter and her family transitioned to their beautiful new home after living with me for more than a year. And now I am an empty nester. I am so proud of them and for them. They deserve this! It was quite different coming home to a quiet home though—a big adjustment. I kept busy working on my book and a few other home projects. Solitude—"island time," "mountain time," or "down time"—can help refresh and renew our minds.

Solitude has two definitions: 1) the state or situation of being alone, and 2) a lonely or uninhabited place. Wikipedia gives thorough information in the form of psychological effects and positive/negative effects of solitude. It even points out that times of solitude can be a time of spiritual enlightenment or rest, and also can spark our creativity. Matthew 6:6 reminds us, "But when you pray, go away by yourself, shut the door behind you, and pray to your Father in private. Then your Father, who sees everything, will reward you."

I relate more to the first definition—the state of being alone. I have come to believe that lonely is a state of mind.

Our state of mind is dependent on what we feed our minds, who we talk with, and what we do. It's also what you read and watch. Lysa TerKeurst says it best. "The mind feasts on what it focuses on. What consumes my thinking will be the making or breaking of my identity (p. 23)." It's not about who we are now, in this season of our life. It's about who we are in HIM. He loves us where we are, but He guides us to who He has designed us to be as we seek Him.

I will sum up my thoughts on solitude from my new read, *Uninvited* by Lisa TerKeurst:

> *I don't have to figure my present circumstances out. I don't have to fill the silence left behind in another person's absence. I don't have to know all the whys and what-ifs. All I have to do is trust. So in quiet humility and without a personal agenda, I make the decision to let God sort it all out. I sit quietly in His presence and simply say, God, I want your truth to be the loudest voice in my life. Correct me. Comfort me. Come closer still. And I will trust. God, you are good at being God.*

In our times of solitude, surrender to His word, His goodness, and trust in who He is. Don't allow the enemy to let you wallow in pity during this time. Get involved in a church, a community or Life group, volunteer, serve others. Be blessed today by blessing someone else.

HOW ARE YOU BLESSING OTHERS? ARE YOU SPENDING TIME alone with God in fellowship? What is your status with Him in service?

FAITH WILL FIND YOU

Lake D'arbonne in Farmerville, LA   Credit: Beth Waldron

SPIN

Do you remember the Sit 'n Spins we played on as children? I am stealing this from Jennie Allen's series, *Stuck*: "Fear, worry, and anxiety plagued me. We sit and spin the most about the things we care the most about. The things that matter most to us." It's so true. When we lack the ability or desire to trust the Lord with every part of our life and trust in Him, it causes us anxiety and stress. We sit and allow our minds to spin out of control too much over the things we cannot control.

Matthew 6: 25-34 reminds to never be worried about our life, for all that we need will be provided: food, water, clothing—everything our body needs. It asks us to look at all the birds—do you think they worry about their existence? They don't plant or reap or store up food, yet your heavenly Father provides them each with food. Aren't you much more valuable to your Father than they? Then comes the big message: Which one of you could add anything to your life by worrying? It goes on to compare our clothing to the beautiful flowers of the field. He notes, "They don't work or toil. Where is our faith?" He asks. It goes on to command us to forsake our worries, for God knows what our bodies need. We are told to chase after the realm of God's kingdom and the righteousness that proceeds from him. And THEN all the less important things will be given to us in abundance. What a promise! Again, we are reminded to refuse to worry about tomorrow. Live one day at a time. Tomorrow will take care of itself! (Matthew 6: 25-34).

Wouldn't it be amazing if we could actually do this?

I propose that we spend the majority of our time doing what we feel the most successful at. If we are a workaholic, it is because we feel that's what we are good at or at least better at than some other areas of our life. We pull away from the areas in our life in which we struggle, be it relationships, attending social events or church. We have all been guilty of hurting those we love at times when we are trying to figure ourselves out. Isn't it strange that no matter our age, we have things in our lives that we are still trying to wrap our heads around? Each of us has something we want to improve or make better—for me there are several. All of my life is a work in progress. I don't pretend to have arrived in any area of my life.

Psalm 19:7 tells us "God's Word is perfect in every way; how it revives our souls! His laws lead us to truth, and his ways change the simple into wise."

Is your life spinning out of control? Let us not allow the enemy to spin our life out of control. We must cling to His word, His promises, His faithfulness, His love, His mercy, His grace. Step out today and do something different. Change your pattern. Change your direction. Let go of wondering about tomorrow and let God lead and guide.

JEANANNE OLDHAM

Too many of us operate from a place of doing the same thing over and over again and expecting different results. We don't change the pattern of how we do things but expect the outcome to be different. Why do we do that? How can we live a worry-free life? Only in Christ is that possible.

STATUS

People may ask or wonder, what's your status? We have economic status, status quo, and relationship status. Let's touch on that last one for now. There are just a few choices on Facebook to choose from: Single, Engaged, Married, In a relationship, In a civil union, In a domestic partnership, In an open partnership, Separated, Divorced, Widowed, or It's complicated. I personally like that one. It keeps everyone guessing.

Most people notice when someone changes their Facebook status. Although sometimes people don't realize until they begin to see a change in your posts that something has inherently changed. With all relationships—family, friends, loved ones, spouses, boyfriend or girlfriend—relationships have to be nurtured. If not, they can become strained or doubt can slip in.

One book that may assist couples to understand what is important to your mate is *The Five Love Languages* by Gary Chapman. The five languages of love, according to Chapman are words of affirmation, quality time, receiving gifts, acts of service, and physical touch. Another online survey suggests the top three priorities in a relationship are Honesty , Communication, and Commitment. This got me thinking about how all these are essential to an effective relationship with God as well. Are we honest with God about who we really are? I mean, there's not really anything we can hide from Him. What about regular communication? Do we take time to commune with God? How often? Do we listen more than we talk? Are we committed to Him, helping to grow the Kingdom of God?

Colossians 3:11 reminds us, "In this new creation life, your nationality makes no difference, or your ethnicity, education, or economic status—they matter nothing. For it is Christ that means everything as he lives in every one of us!"

What is your relationship status with God? We all want to belong. We were made to belong and be loved. Unfortunately, most all of us have gone looking for love in the wrong places before. You may have owned the Urban Cowboy cassette or seen that movie in 1980.

I was lookin' for love in all the wrong places,
Lookin' for love in too many faces,
Searchin' their eyes and lookin' for traces
Of what I'm dreamin' of...

The most important thing in anyone's life is their relationship with God. It took me many years to learn this, although I knew it or had already been taught it on some level. This MOST important relationship assures your future in eternity, but also it determines the quality of your life here on earth. Our relationship with our maker is just as important and necessary as our need for food, water, and the air we breathe. Without it, something will always be missing in our lives.

There's the physical touch—this could be the intimacy of

praise and worship, or our utterings when we are out of words to pray, crying out to Him with our raw hurt and sometimes agony. 1 Corinthians 12:13 says, "For by one Spirit we all were immersed and mingled into one single body. And no matter our status—Jews or non-Jews, oppressed or free—we are all privileged to drink deeply of the same Holy Spirit."

Unfortunately, when we are not living as we should, other things fill our lives—money, sex, drugs, etc—but they only temporarily hide or cover our needs. The search in those areas is meaningless and none of them will ever satisfy our internal need for a true relationship with God—He is the only thing that will supply our every need. Make sure you keep your status with God current. Keep it real, but intimate. Keep the lines of communication open by talking with Him often each day. Give more than you receive. You will be blessed.

"And it's not just creation. We who have already experienced the first fruits of the Spirit also inwardly groan as we passionately long to experience our full status as God's sons and daughters—including our physical bodies being transformed" (Romans 8:23).

WHAT'S YOUR STATUS WITH GOD TODAY? WHAT ARE WE giving to God? Do we honor Him with words of affirmation? Do we give him quality time each day or maybe only weekly or monthly or less? Do we honor Him with our gifts, as in serving and using the gifts He has blessed us with? That also relates to acts of service—what do we do for others?

SURVIVAL

When we hear the word survival, we may think of the survival of the fittest. We may think of those who survived after a tragic accident or injury from a wreck, accident, or natural disaster. We think about survival skills that we may need one day—hunting, fishing, living in the elements—if need be. Thankfully, we have cancer survivors and many who have overcome the bondage of addiction.

Other types of survival skills include the mental capacity to be able to withstand the attacks of the enemy or negativity or rejection. Our hardships or struggles give us strength we never knew we had. They determine our perseverance. Can we stick it out? Can we withstand the pressure? Can we believe in our hearts and still speak with our mouths what we know is true or do we doubt that we can make it? Are we survivors?

Acts 27:44 tells us that "the rest all managed to survive by clinging to planks and broken pieces of the ship, so that everyone scrambled to the shore uninjured."

So many of us don't talk about our brokenness. We hide

the hurt, the shame, the damage that we have experienced. It does not matter if we caused our own ruin by our poor decisions or if we were an innocent bystander. We could be the victim, culprit, predator, or instigator. The shattering of our hearts and emotions still damages our self-esteem. We are hanging on to what's left. We are hanging on for dear life.

The Bible doesn't speak directly about survival per se, instead the term overcome is used. Jesus said in John 16:33 NKJV, "...In this world you will have tribulation; but be of good cheer, I have overcome the world."

We can be overcomers because Jesus was an overcomer. The Lord has provided a way for the believer to be victorious over every foe he faces. Some days, weeks, months—honestly, some years—we just survive and barely. We muddle through. I have been there, wondering if I would make it. We feel defeated, if only on the inside. Our faces and our words won't reveal how wrecked we feel on the inside. We are masterful at hiding our damaged thoughts. But in HIM we have hope. Sometimes we just survive, but God has called us to not only survive, but to THRIVE.

The Bible tells is in Psalm 1:1-3 ESV, "Blessed is the man who walks not in the counsel of the wicked, nor stands in the way of sinners, nor sits in the seat of scoffers; but his delight is in the law of the LORD, and on his law he meditates day and night. He is like a tree planted by streams of water that yields its fruit in its season, and its leaf does not wither. In all that he does, he prospers." He perseveres, he thrives!

How are you surviving today? What are your survival techniques? Don't you want to thrive instead of only surviving?

SUPERHERO

I went to the movie theater one night with my grandsons and daughter-in-law to see *The Incredibles*. In the beginning of the movie, superheroes were illegal. The first encounter where the family with superpowers tried to help the city wound up costing them their livelihood. The authorities only saw what went wrong and not the lives that were saved or how the efforts prevented the situation from having a different ending. The Incredibles had their identity tested. They knew they had secret weapons that others did not have, but initially it was not appreciated. The story takes a turn when Elastigirl finds an advocate who has the right connections to get her recognized and involved again in the superhero world.

This got me thinking about our identity as Christians. We too sometimes are not recognized by our potential, but why? Maybe we don't allow ourselves to see ourselves as sons and daughters of a most high KING. Shawn Smith, pastor of Pointblank International, made the following comments during one sermon. I suggest you read them more than once to allow them to soak in.

1. Some of us are going through status-changing battles. We are not going through something, but to something.
2. If you don't hunger for more, you will settle for less.
3. Always remember that God knows something about us that we don't know. He knows our full potential.
4. The recognition of your identity gets your fight back. Sometimes you just need to tell the devil who you are!

Psalm 68:23 tells us, "For my people will be the conquerors; they will soon have you under their feet. They will crush you until there is nothing left!" And in Romans 8:37 we are reminded, "Yet even in the midst of all these things, we triumph over them all, for God has made us to be more than conquerors, and his demonstrated love is our glorious victory over everything!"

"Greater is He that is within me than he that is within the world" (1 John 4:4).

Yes, everything! Nothing left that we cannot conquer. Who is your superhero today? What is your identity in Christ? Are you living life to your full potential?

SURRENDER

I am a planner and a fixer. In my mind, and most of the time, I plan things out. I am a list maker. I love to be able to check items off once completed. I even have a bucket list of things I would like to do before I kick the bucket. But what happens when some of those plans don't work out?

I once had a plan in my mind, one I believed was orchestrated by God Himself until it was muted, deleted—and SNAP, just like that, a rug was jerked out from under my feet. My boyfriend of almost six months broke off our relationship to be with another woman. I mean, it really sent me for a loop. I cried. I wailed. I got on the floor and prayed to God to heal my brokenness. I talked with close friends about it. I wrote about it. I prayed about it some more. And I cried some more. Until peace came. Finally.

As much as I had received freedom from my last marriage where I was beaten down, undervalued, and made to feel unworthy to be loved and appreciated, this relationship had given me so much joy, so much so that others noticed a remarkable difference in me and told me so. It restored my hope that I am lovable and God is growing me into a person someone will appreciate, respect, and love just as Christ loved the Church. I began to see my value and my Godly purpose. That type of bond should bring commitment to a union in which Christ is the cornerstone—a partnership of three—a strand of three that cannot be broken, compromised, or abandoned.

Yet, just as disappointed and hurt as I was, I was also grateful that I received God's divine intervention. I came to understand the relationship was not the one God intended to be a strand of three for me. Still, it left me feeling "not enough." Not chosen.

My first relationship after my divorce caught me off guard. He searched me out. It had been over twenty years since I had been a part of the dating scene and what I found was that dating now is NOT for the faint of heart. In this most recent failure to launch, the lesson for me was surrender. Surrender or death to my plans, my hopes, my dreams and total submission to God's plan for my life. From now on I am yielding in order to grow more in Him and give of myself to others. Others who choose me. Others who value me. Others who take actions instead of making empty promises. Others who are honest and transparent. Because I too am transparent and honest and loving and open about who I am and how deeply I care.

"I pray with great faith for you, because I'm fully convinced that the One who began this glorious work in you will faithfully continue the process of maturing you and will put his finishing touches to it until the unveiling of our Lord Jesus Christ" (Philippians 1:6).

God has a reason for our struggles—surrender. He has a purpose for our pain—healing. He has a refuge for our rejection—acceptance. There is purpose in the timing—trust.

How are you doing in trusting God's timing? How is your healing coming along? Are you consulting the Master counselor for your acceptance? You are enough. Believe you are who He says you are.

TRANSFORMATION

When we give our heart to Jesus, we become a new person. One with new words and actions. Our transformation begins that day but is a constant work in progress. Depending on the number of years we have lived up to that point, the lifestyle we lived may influence how long it takes for us to make a total transformation. But we never really arrive until the end of our time here on earth.

There are many things in nature that are transformed. I think of the tadpole turning to a frog. Transformation for humans is similar to a life cycle of some insects. All insects change in form as they grow—through metamorphosis or in size. Butterflies and moths undergo complete metamorphosis in which there are four distinct stages: egg, larva (caterpillar), pupa (chrysalis), and adult. I think of the miraculous process from start to finish. Even the caterpillar eating milkweed so that nothing wants to eat it is part of God's divine plan of creation. All of this four-stage plan is accomplished in a six- to eight-week lifespan. Amazing!

God also has a divine plan for each of us. In 2 Corinthians

5:17 KJV it says, "Therefore if anyone is in Christ, he is a new creature; the old things passed away; behold, new things have come." Just think of the creative plan for the short life of a butterfly. How much more important is our life than a butterfly? God does so much work for our divine plan behind the scenes. He weaves people and events in and out of our lives. Sometimes He keeps us in a cocoon unto Himself to do a work in us. Thank you, Pat Hutson Bruner for this reminder. He directs our path as much as we allow Him. However, we still have our free will that comes in to play.

There is a great message from the Are *You There?* series by Brother Dallas Witt that asks, "Have you ever been in a place where you didn't think God was hearing you?"

Sure, we all have. Even though we have faith, we still sometimes have doubt. Doubt that God is not hearing us or that He has forgotten about us—although we know the complete opposite is true in both cases. Deuteronomy 31:6 (NKJV) says, "Be strong and of good courage, do not fear nor be afraid of them; for the Lord your God, He is the One who goes with you. He will not leave you nor forsake you."

Transformation in Christ does not come for us unless we allow it. It won't happen on its own either. We must be open and intimate with our Abba Father. We must seek Him. What are you saying to me today, God? What are you doing? Our new life is no longer ours. Others should see His life, His grace, His mercy, His goodness in us. Galatians 2:20 TPT tell us:

> *My old identity has been co-crucified with Messiah and no longer lives; for the nails of his cross crucified me with him. And now the essence of this new life is no longer mine, for the Anointed One lives his life through me—we live in union as one! My new life is*

empowered by the faith of the Son of God who loves me so much that he gave himself for me, and dispenses his life into mine!

Staying in tune with Jesus is a choice, a free will option, if you will. The ability to be able to connect with God is available to us. The enemy wants to keep slipping us the bait. He wants us to doubt or forget God's promises. Our accuser is relentless.

We pray for God to send someone and He says, "I already did. I sent my only Son and then I sent the Holy Spirit." Now we as Children of God have a work to do. Have you heard Matthew West's song, "Do Something?" Check it out. We are called to grow the kingdom of God by loving and serving others. What are we doing daily to fulfill our promise to God?

"And to be transformed as you embrace the glorious Christ-within as your new life and live in union with him! For God has recreated you all over again in his perfect righteousness, and you now belong to him in the realm of true holiness" (Ephesians 4:24).

"He saved us, not on the basis of deeds which we have done in righteousness, but according to His mercy, by the washing of regeneration and renewing by the Holy Spirit" (Titus 3:5 NASB).

TALK TO GOD EACH DAY. ASK, "LORD, WHAT ARE YOU saying? What are you doing in my life? What would you have me do?

TRUST

Life is filled with disappointment. And during those times, the enemy sows seeds of distrust with thoughts of mistrust. Disappointment and discouragement become the breeding ground for Satan's lies to take root. The enemy takes every opportunity to step in when our defenses are down. When we are sad or mad or broken or hurt or discontented or scared or overwhelmed or just plain stuck. We sometimes refer to being stuck in a rut. We tend to repeat our patterns of the past unless we are intentional about change. Back to insanity—doing the same thing over and over again and expecting different results.

Has the devil ever said to you, "I told you so!" Maybe when you had rebuked his lies about who you are or when a relationship was not going to working out. You were unworthy to be loved. You would never have a successful relationship. These are the same types of lies he told Eve in the garden of Eden: *God is holding out on you. You can't trust Him.* But Psalm 18:30 tells us, "As for God, his way is perfect: the Lord's word is flawless; He shields all who take refuge in him."

Here's what I've learned about God:

He is always good.
He always tells the truth.
He wants what's best for me.
I can trust Him.

Proverbs 3:5-6 ESV reminds us to "trust in the Lord with all your heart, and do not lean on your own understanding. In all your ways acknowledge Him, and He will make straight your paths."

The good thing about disappointment and hurt is that it means you cared, you tried, and the lesson is that it has taught you something. Some chapters have to close without closure. Sometimes people are afforded the opportunity to have a do-over. Some of us have to accept the end of certain chapters and move on.

Take my ex-boyfriend and current friend, Eddie. (Yes, please somebody take him—he's a mess.) Someone broke his heart many years ago and they now have an opportunity to rekindle the relationship. This is a rarity.

He and I will always be friends. Here's what I learned from our time together: There are men chasing after God's heart who will attend church with you and pray with you and over you. They read their Bible and mentor others. This was something I never had—EVER! It has given me hope. (Yes, and some sadness for me, but happiness for him.) Joy comes in the morning, you know. Christian friends are hard to come by, especially male friends—they are difficult to find.

One day, God will bring me the answers I desire. In His time.

"So we are convinced that every detail of our lives is continually woven together to fit into God's perfect plan of bringing good into our lives, for we are his lovers who have been called to fulfill his designed purpose" (Romans 8:28).

WHAT HAS HAPPENED IN YOUR LIFE THAT HAS LEFT YOU wondering if God has abandoned you? He has not. Talk with him. Allow him to do a mighty work in your life. Have doors closed that caught you off guard? When you don't get why things are taken from you, seek God out and simply trust Him. It may have been protection that you will only understand later. Have doors closed that you don't understand?

VESSEL

A vessel is a large ship or a container that holds liquid. I found a sermon by D.L. Moody titled, "Useful Vessel." It has a great message about the requirements of being a useful vessel for God. However, think about what guides us as a vessel and why so many do not feel worthy to be used. Events and influences—good and bad—have created the person we each are today. There's a saying, "Life is 10% what happens to us and 90% how we react to it." So many times we want to blame our circumstances instead of clinging to His word and going to Him in prayer. It is essential to pray, have faith, and believe—in every circumstance!

Romans 8:38-39 tells us:

So now I live with the confidence that there is nothing in the universe with the power to separate us from God's love. I'm convinced that His love will triumph over death, life's troubles, fallen angels, or dark rulers in the heavens. There is nothing in our present or future circumstances that can weaken his love.

JEANANNE OLDHAM

There is no power above or beneath us—no power that could ever be found in the universe that can distance us from God's passionate love, which is lavished upon us through our Lord Jesus, the Anointed One!

"You're as real to me as bedrock beneath my feet, like a castle on a cliff, my forever firm fortress, my mountain of hiding, my pathway of escape, my tower of rescue where none can reach me. My secret strength and shield around me, you are salvation's ray of brightness shining on the hillside, always the champion of my cause" (Psalm 18:2).

I am grateful to be His vessel and grateful and honored to be used for His glory.

WHAT HAPPENS TO US IN OUR LIVES MAY MAKE IT SEEM THAT the devil is trying to hijack our destination, but with God steering our ship the journey will be successful. Don't allow your circumstances today to keep you from communing with God. Ask Him how He can use you as a vessel today. How do you see God using your talents and character to give back to others?

VOICES

Sometimes at night I sit outside a while just to soak in the calmness of the crickets chirping and some classic country tunes. It makes for a peaceful night's sleep once I settle in.

I TRY TO CHALLENGE MYSELF TO WRITE ORIGINAL THOUGHTS and use scripture accordingly. But sometimes I check out other writing and devotions.

Sarah Young's "Jesus Calling Daily" devotion is about listening to birds calling to one another and how God speaks to us in a variety of mediums—sights, sounds, thoughts, impressions, scriptures. His communication with us is not limited to these. Everyone has their own preferences—I love music of all kinds, but I feel such a connection when I hear praise and worship or gospel music.

Our part of this two-way dialogue with God is to be attentive to His voice or messages in whatever form he gives us. The point was also made that we find Him not only in the good things like nature and music, but also in the grief-stricken faces of tragedy and sickness. He can take the deepest sorrow and weave it into a pattern for good. Romans 8:28 supports this when it says all things work together for those that love God and are fitting into His plans. He is masterful at taking our brokenness and making a masterpiece.

"My sheep listen to my voice; I know them, and they follow me" (John 10:27 KJV).

"You will Seek and find me when you seek me with all your heart" (Jeremiah 28:13 NIV).

Won't you seek Him today with your whole being? He wants to use you? Never doubt that.

WAIT

I have already publicly and privately admitted that I am an impatient person, and so it is a constant work in progress to make improvements in that area of my life. It is OK to admit our weaknesses, because in our weakness He is strong. And God will bring others into our lives to fill the void that we have. We are all broken together—the body of Christ.

At one point, I was dealing with a personal issue in regard to being patient. While sitting in church listening to Pastor Chris Witt of LifeChurch.LA (in Ruston and Jonesboro) preach on being a warrior for Christ, I wrote the word "WAIT" across the end of the margin in all caps. God spoke to me. He said, "You have asked for this all your life, now because you are listening to ME, I am trying it to make it happen in your life, so why are trying to take the lead? Wait on this situation. Stop trying to be in control. Surrender to me and the Holy Spirit, and let someone else have the lead."

Wait for the Lord; be strong and take heart and wait for the Lord (Psalm 27:14).

Many of us are walking in faith today because of the

prayers our parents and grandparents and even great-grandparents prayed over our lives or even their future generations. We tried doing things "our way," but that did not work out so well. We have all heard the phrase, "Hold your horses" or "Like a bull in a china shop." Does your life seem like either of those? Are we in a constant state of crisis, running around, wildly attacking those problems . . . without even seeking God's guidance? If we are constantly running from one potential solution to the next, we may miss our lesson or even our blessing.

God promises that our future with Him is not like our past. Praise God! He is shaping us with His capable hands and is preparing you and me for all that is coming. Set your eyes on Him, and He will never disappoint. You will not be taken captive by the fear of this age.

Promises long forgotten will now be fulfilled. Rest in the understanding that He knows your future and has marked out every step, bringing you closer to Him and deeper into his glory, until finally, you will awake with his likeness.

"As for me, because I am innocent, I will see your face—Until I see you for who you really are. Then I will awaken with your form and be fully satisfied, fulfilled in the revelation of your glory in me (Psalm 17:15).

Won't you allow God to use your mess as a message of hope for others? Your trials will become your testimony of His goodness and mercy. What can you share with someone today that will encourage them on their journey?

WHO KNEW?

A close relative told me that she never knew I was ever depressed; she always thought I was a really happy person. My response was, "Yes, I am very good at hiding it." Granted, when I am around people that consistently make me laugh and smile, the subject about how sad I am on the inside does not come up. I block it out and hide it from others, even those I am closest to.

As a school leader, I cannot allow my personal issues to affect the job I do. To a certain extent, it does affect my work from time to time, but overall I am still responsible to be the person in charge and make decisions and put out fires (not literally) on a daily basis.

Since I have opened up about the shadows I face in my life or have faced, I have had so many people reach out to tell me that they needed to hear that, that they are facing or have faced depression for an extended length of time. We look at people from the outside and never know what is happening on the inside. I have had several people reach out, people that I believe have it so much more together than me.

Please, please, please be cognizant of those around you.

Don't just say, "How are you?" They tell you they're fine and you both move on. Slow down, take a moment to give them a hug or say, "No, really how are you doing? What's going on in your life?"

We are all living in a fast-paced world and day after day we wake up and think, *Wow, I wish I had told them how much they meant to me. I wish I had said those three little words that we all want to hear.* I promise this, we will never lose someone we care for and wish we had said less to them—it's always more.

Who knew? We know One who knew and knows all about what's going on in our minds. Jesus knows. We cannot hide how we feel from Him. He is our hope! Psalm 17:8 reminds us, "Keep me [in Your affectionate care, protect me] as the apple of Your eye; Hide me in the [protective] shadow of Your wings. We are the apple of His eye. We should hide away in Him. Find time alone to abide in Him each day. You will not regret what peace and joy and comfort His peace and everlasting hope brings."

Then you would trust [with confidence], because there is hope; You would look around you and rest securely" (Job 11:18).

WHO KNOWS WHAT IS GOING ON IN YOUR HEART AND MIND? What are you hiding today? Do you have a friend you can share your troubles with? Remember that God is always there for you. He is a great listener. When you tune in to Him, he will speak. Will you listen?

WHY?

There are times when people come into our life and we may not understand the purpose, but God does. He knows the why. Let the words of this song be an encouragement to you when times get hard. Look around you and give thanks for the blessings in your life. It will build your faith even through seasons of dust.

"If your faith remains strong, even while surrounded by life's difficulties, you will continue to experience the untold blessings of God! True happiness comes as you pass the test with faith, and receive the victorious crown of life promised to every lover of God!" (James 1:12).

JEANANNE OLDHAM

I Don't Know Why

By: Seth Easterling

Some days this old life gets hard.
Sometimes I get lost in the dark.
But I know if I keep the faith He'll show me the way.
Sometimes I get so sad and He reminds me that life ain't that bad.
I look around and see all the blessings I have.

CHORUS:
And I don't know why I feel so sorry for myself sometimes.
When I'm a born-again child of the King.
Heaven's angels are waiting on me.
There's a mansion on a street of gold that bears my name.
I'm gonna sit down by the river of life, talk with my loved ones and laugh for a while
Together with the Saints as we all sing Amazing Grace.

WIDE OPEN SPACES

There is an old familiar song out there, "Wide Open Spaces," sung by the Dixie Chicks. I sang this song back in 1999 with Rhonda and Duane Satcher in our short stint as a band. We had three gigs and then he got sick with cancer and passed away. Our singing together was a time that I will always remember fondly. The lyrics begin:

She needs wide open spaces
Room to make her big mistakes
She needs new faces
She knows the high stakes

Basically, it is about a girl striking out to find her dreams. Maybe leaving small town America for some metropolis where she can spread her wings. In contrast, there's a Facebook page, "Wide Open Spaces," that addresses anything and everything concerning the great outdoors—hunting and fishing. It is based in Austin, Texas, and is an informational site to improve the outdoor enthusiast experiences.

This term, "wide open spaces," brought to mind how the Lord expands our territory. He brings people into our lives for specific reasons or He takes us places we may not want to go or think we would ever visit. Sometimes people grow us, teach us, or just carry us through whatever is going on in our life.

In 1 Chronicles 4:10 NASB it reads, "Now Jabez called on the God of Israel, saying, 'Oh that You would bless me indeed and enlarge my border, and that Your hand might be with me, and that You would keep me from harm that it may not pain me!' And God granted him what he requested."

In the history of Israel, Jabez lived just after the dividing of the Promised Land into portions for each tribe. As he looked over the spread his family had passed down to him, he calculated the potential and made a decision: "Everything you've put under my care, O Lord, take it and enlarge it." If we pray for God to enlarge our territory, we are asking Him to enlarge our lives in some way in order to make a bigger impact for Him. It may bring more responsibility. It may require more dedication in your service. It may take your life in a different direction. God has trusted us as stewards of that which He gives us. That is not limited to land or property we own. It's more about growing spiritually and getting out into those wide open spaces of limitless service to enlarge the kingdom of God.

Some people believe that when others openly claim their dedication to Jesus, they are claiming they are perfect or believe they are above others who have not made that decision yet. It is really just the opposite. We put our pants on just like everyone else each day—we just might be smiling or praying or praising the Lord for waking us up one more day so we can give Him thanks and honor and glory.

The difference is that we as Christians know that every day the devil will try to steal our joy and plant doubt in our minds about who we are in Christ. We just have the assurance that we are striving to be a better person every day, to do more for others, and for others to see Him in us.

I had a memory pop up on my Facebook page one night. It said at the same time last year, I had beat a hard level on a computer game. It was during a time when God was dealing with me about how much time I was wasting playing computer games and that I could be doing something more productive. I went back and forth with God about how I just needed this game to help me decompress or wind down. Well, a few months later, I stopped playing computer games or even watching much TV and began reading and writing.

You see, that is one way God has enlarged my territory. God is using every skeleton in my closet and every dark cloud I passed through to help encourage others. It's like, *Hey, she made it and so can I!* No matter what we face, remember God promises joy does come in the morning.

No matter what you are facing today, He is there for you. Look around you and be thankful for all the good in your life. I also want to encourage you to give back to others. I know you say, *I am too depressed, too down and out, or I just don't like being around others.* I know—I have been there. Stop hiding, get out of your shell. Yes, fake it until you make it. You will be blessed by blessing others. Give it a try. There are so many wide open spaces that need your smile—somebody, somewhere needs you. Look outward and not inward.

"From my distress I called upon the LORD; The LORD answered me and set me in a large place" (Psalm 118:5 NASB).

JEANANNE OLDHAM

In what way can you see God enlarging your territory? Your circle of friends? How can you serve others even during difficult times?

EPILOGUE

This journey began at my birth. I know that each and every part of who I am today developed over years of mishaps and missteps. I have had many of those. We all have. Some of us more than others. The difference is what we do with them.

Do we hide them away in a shoebox out of shame, never to share? Or do we use them to help us make a better life? A life with purpose and fulfillment. Do we use them to encourage and support others? Do we reflect on them each time we are about to judge someone else? Do we remember them to keep us humble? Do we write them either in journals or maybe pen some lyrics of songs never to be sung?

Although sharing my personal and very raw feelings has not always been easy, God gave me a vision. A vision that includes helping others that feel the same way. Inadequate. Sad. Depressed. Lonely. Disappointed. Heartbroken. These writings were birthed out of my own failures that left me feeling not enough. Unloved and unworthy. But God used my brokenness and gave me blessings through writing about them. He used my inadequacies to build my confidence not with what others say or think about me, but who HE says I am in Christ. I am the daughter of a King who loves me endlessly. Recklessly. And unconditionally. For all time.

My hope is that these words give you promise of God's belief in who you are in Him. My prayer is that you believe it's never too late. Never too late to find your purpose. Never too late to make a difference in the lives of others. Never too late to give your heart to God. Never too late to be given a gift that can be used to bring Him honor and praise.

Faith is something that is practiced. Not just on Sunday. Or even daily, but hour by hour and minute by minute. We are tested and we are tried. Faith is putting into action what we believe in our heart. It is praising God through the prickles of this life. It is worshiping through the worries. It is praying in our love language when our tears and words have gone stale and dry. Faith grows during adversity. Trials will come but be persistent in knowing that He is in control and always is walking us through whatever seems might break us for good. Cling to His word. Know He is a good, good Father . . . always. He never leaves or forsakes us—ever! He believes in you and has a purpose and a reason for your life. Seek Him out. He is waiting. Get ready to soar.

"You satisfy my every desire with good things. You've supercharged my life so that I soar again like a flying eagle in the sky" (Psalm 103:5)!

"So my conclusion is this: Many are the sorrows and frustrations of those who don't come clean with God. But when you trust in the Lord for forgiveness, his wrap-around love will surround you" (Psalm 32:10).

ACKNOWLEDGMENTS

• To my parents: Marvin and Jean Oldham, thank you for bringing me up in a Christian home and making me go to church—even when I didn't want to. Thank you for flooding my life with music and laughter and sewing and photography and horses and cows and sports and love and food and family get-togethers.

• To my children: Ty (Lacey), Paige (DJ), and Lyle (Ashley), thank you for loving me despite all the mistakes I have made. By the way, I may not be through just yet. Thanks for all the times you have been there for me when I needed you. Thanks for sharing your sweet families with me. You are all such a joy to be around. I am so proud of each and every one of you, and the decisions that you have made in your lives that make me one grateful momma. Always keep God first in your heart and in your marriage. It is a lesson I can't go back and fix. My prayer is that through my transgressions you learned what not to do and can have a full and happy life.

• To my brother, Marley and sister, Judy and their spouses, Linda and James: Thank you for all the jokes—told and played on me, hugs, phone calls, love, patience, and spoiling of your baby sister. I love you all so much and am blessed beyond measure to call you my family.

• My life would not be what it is today without the support and prayers of my church family over the past six years. Special thanks is not enough to say how blessed I am to have LifeChurch.LA in Ruston, LA, in my corner. You are forever in my heart!

• Thank you to my friends, both near and far, and old and new. For checking on me when you knew I needed it. For words of encouragement and guidance. For donations and gifts and trips and laughter. For hugs and tears over the good, the bad, and the ugly. For workouts and swims and listening ears. For fewer broken limbs. My friends are the best—Nancy, Kristi, Sheri, Leisa—you girls are amazing. I don't know what I would do without you!

• To every guy that ever broke my heart and made me cry. I am over it! Really! You helped shape who I am. Those lessons learned made me a better person. Heartaches gave me a reason to write about my feelings. Thank you, I am now a published author!

• To every person that ever told me I am beautiful or talented or kind. You made me feel special and worthy and loved. Thank you! I needed to hear it just when you told me.

• And last, but certainly not least to my J-HES faculty/staff who have walked with me through the changes in my life. Thank you for your understanding. Thank you for your patience. Thank you for allowing me to be a part of your lives. It has been the best decision I ever made and you will forever be a part of my life and memories.

My Family: Christmas 2018 Credit: Kacey Stringer Photography

Me with my mother, father, sister and brother in 2000. Credit: Delores Danley

ABOUT THE AUTHOR

Jeananne Oldham is a veteran educator who has worked in education for over twenty years in a variety of roles: teacher, educational consultant, instructional coach, and principal. The focus of her work has been in the area of literacy—with a heart for struggling readers.

Jeananne's goal in life is to make a difference in the lives of others by encouraging them to live their life fully through adventure, travel, and creativity. She considers herself an encourager and enjoys serving others in her church and community. She also enjoys spending time with her family and friends at home, especially in her pool and outside.

Made in the USA
Columbia, SC
17 May 2021